WHAT'S U
JAPANESE
RESTAURANTS

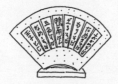

WHAT'S WHAT IN JAPANESE RESTAURANTS

A Guide to Ordering, Eating, and Enjoying

Robb Satterwhite

KODANSHA INTERNATIONAL
Tokyo • New York • London

PHOTO CREDITS
Front cover: Ikuo Nonaka. Back cover: Ienohikari Photo Service /American Photo Library (top), Photo Library Myojyo/American Photo Library (bottom).
Photo insert: Plates 2, 6–27, and 29 by Hiroya Yoshimori. Plate 5 by Ben Simmons.

Published by Kodansha International Ltd., 17–14 Otowa 1-chome, Bunkyo-ku, Tokyo 112–8652, and Kodansha America, Inc.

Distributed in the United States by Kodansha America, Inc., 575 Lexington Avenue, New York, New York 10022, and in the United Kingdom and continental Europe by Kodansha Europe Ltd., 95 Aldwych, London WC2B 4JF.

First edition, 1988
First mass market paperback, 1996
02 03 04 05   9 8 7 6

LCC 87–82865
ISBN 4–7700–2086–4

www.thejapanpage.com

CONTENTS

Preface   7

Introduction   17

A Guide to Japanese Pronunciation   21

PART I

ABOUT JAPANESE RESTAURANTS
The Art of Japanese Cooking   26
Restaurant Customs   28
Phrases for Ordering in Japanese   33
Recognizing Specialty Restaurants   40
Reading Numbers and Basic Vocabulary Terms   45
Using the Sample Menus   48

PART II

SPECIALTY RESTAURANTS AND THEIR MENUS
Sushi   52
Unagi (Eel)   61
Fugu (Blowfish)   64
Tempura   66
Soba and Udon (Buckwheat and Thick White Noodles)   71
Tonkatsu (Pork Cutlets)   78
Kushiage (Skewered Foods)   81
Yakitori (Grilled Chicken)   84
Kamameshi (Rice Dishes)   89

Nabemono (Quick-Cooked Stews)   92
Sukiyaki and Shabu-shabu (Beef Hotpot Dishes)   96
Oden (Fish-Cake Stews)   99
Okonomiyaki (Japanese Savory Pancakes)   102
Teppanyaki (Grilled Steaks)   105
Izakaya (Pubs)   107
Robatayaki (Japanese Barbecue)   114
Regional Specialties   115
Nihon-ryōri (General Japanese Cuisine)   120
Yakiniku (Korean Barbecue)   128
Ramen and Chinese Food   132
Other Specialty Restaurants   140
Japanese Desserts   141
Coffee Shops   145
Boxed Lunches and Food Delivery   150
Drinking in Japan   154

Japanese Food Vocabulary and Glossary   161

Preface

One of the most exciting parts of traveling to a foreign country is being able to experience the local culture by sampling the native cuisine. Japanese cuisine reflects many traditional aspects of Japanese culture; the significance of the changing seasons, the importance of the art of presentation, and the historical relationship of the Japanese people with the sea are a few examples. Even more important than culture, though, is flavor, and Japanese cuisine offers a dazzling variety of delicious dishes and unique cooking styles.

Until now, a major obstacle to exploring this exciting food in its native habitat has been the difficulty of reading Japanese menus. Unlike European languages, where one can get by with just a pocket dictionary, written Japanese uses thousands of different characters, and many years of intense study are required for one to master them all.

The purpose of this book, then, is to act as both a translator and a tour guide to the world of Japanese food, explaining not only what to order but also how to order it. By referring to the sample menus in the book, visitors to Japan (and foreign residents as well) can skip years of language study and immediately read and understand the greater part of an actual Japanese menu, even if they can't speak a word of Japanese.

Besides serving as a handy menu translator, *What's What in Japanese Restaurants* will introduce you to the many interesting specialty cuisines of Japan, explaining the different cooking styles and the various native ingredients used. It offers insights into culinary customs and history, as well as into some of the finer points of food preparation (for example, what distinguishes really good tempura from ordinary, run-of-the-mill tempura). Also included are an extensive phrase section that can be used in restaurants, and a special glossary section filled with food terms and their corresponding Japanese characters, making this a comprehensive reference source as well as an easy-to-use introductory guide.

So wherever you go in Japan, I hope this book will serve as a trustworthy companion on many happy eating adventures.

[The author wishes to gratefully thank the following persons for their help in the preparation of the manuscript: His editors at Kodansha International, Okinori Murata and Stephen Comee, as well as Jonathan Dunham, Suwako Endo, Hirokazu Ishige, Richard Jeffery, Steven Nethercott, Ronald Sternberg, Takaaki Sunaga, and Masako Wada.]
Robb Satterwhite

1. A sushi chef presenting a selection of *nigiri-zushi*.

2. An order of *chirashi-zushi*. (See ''Sushi'' chapter.)

3. Exterior view of a pub-style *izakaya* restaurant. (See "Izakaya" chapter.)

4. Interior of a rustic *izakaya* pub.

5. Chef roasting prawns over a charcoal grill, *robata-yaki*-style. (See "Robatayaki" chapter.)

6. Assorted skewers of *yakitori*: grilled chicken, leeks, livers, and Japanese green peppers.

7. A typical assortment of small dishes, served with drinks at an *izakaya* pub.

8. *Sukiyaki:* raw ingredients (rear), and the finished stew (front).
9. *Shabu-shabu:* thinly sliced beef being quick-cooked in boiling stock. (See ''Sukiyaki and Shabu-shabu'' chapter.)

10. A full-course *fugu* (blowfish) dinner.

11. Quick-cooked *nabemono*-style chicken stew. (See ''Nabemono'' chapter.)

12. *Tonkatsu* platter: breaded, deep-fried pork cutlet with sliced cabbage.

13. *Tendon:* prawns fried tempura-style and served over rice. (See "Tempura" chapter.)

14. *Yakiniku* (Korean-style barbecue): vegetables and marinated beef slices on the grill.

15. *Unadon:* grilled eel served over a bowl of rice. (See "Unagi" chapter.)

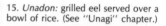

16. A typical assortment of stewed *oden* ingredients.

17. Two styles of serving buckwheat *soba* noodles: cold *zaru-soba* (front) and *kake-soba* in hot broth (rear).

18. and 19. Two varieties of Chinese-style *ramen* noodles.

20. A summer specialty: cold *somen* noodles with various garnishes. (See "Soba" chapter.)

21. Entrance of a Japanese *kappō* restaurant. (See "Nihon-ryori" chapter.)

22. Interior of a traditional *kappō* restaurant. (See "Nihon-ryori" chapter.)

23. Various traditional dishes. (See "Nihon-ryori" chapter.)

24. Counter of a tempura restaurant, with full-course tempura meal.

25. *Maku-no-uchi bento* lunch box, with rice and assorted tidbits of food. (See ''Boxed Lunches and Food Delivery'' chapter.)

26. Deep-fried *kushiage* skewers (rear), and raw ingredients (front).

27. Japanese *wagashi* sweets served with a pot of green tea. (See "Japanese Desserts" chapter.)

28. An assortment of Kyoto-style *wagashi* sweets. (See "Japanese Desserts" chapter.)

29. A variety of Japanese desserts: (clockwise from upper left) *Abekawamochi*, *oshiruko*, warm *zenzai*, and two kinds of *anmitsu*.

Introduction

It has been claimed that Tokyo contains more restaurants than any other city in the world. It's easy to believe, too, since wherever you look in Tokyo there's an incredible profusion of eating places. They're tucked into side streets, nestled under railroad tracks, and grouped together on the upper floors of major department stores. There are several cultural reasons for this proliferation of eateries. In Japanese social situations, for example, it's far more common to meet friends in restaurants, pubs, or coffee shops than it is to entertain at home. Another reason is that many of Japan's favorite foods are troublesome to cook in tiny home kitchens.

Whatever the reasons, the large number of restaurants has led to competition, and competition has led to specialization. Most Japanese restaurants concentrate on only one style of cooking, whether it's tempura, sushi, *yakitori*, or any of a number of other specific cuisines. A few of these cooking styles have become popular in the West, and the most famous dishes, such as sukiyaki and tempura, are quite well known. However, there's also a whole world of great cooking practically unknown outside of Japan, with delicious rewards awaiting the adventurous diner.

Unfortunately, most visitors to Japan (and even many foreign residents) are discouraged from exploring this vast frontier of interesting restaurants, largely due to the difficulty of understanding the menus. Although pointing to the plastic food models in the window or pointing to the plate of the customer at the next table usually works to some extent, these techniques begin to lose their charm rather quickly. As a result, defeated diners soon find themselves always ordering the same two or three dishes with easily pronounceable names, or going to restaurants with English menus, or even frequenting fast-food restaurants. In short, missing out on a lot of interesting food and good eating.

The goal of this book is to change all that, and make Japanese cuisine accessible to everyone. First of all, the book can be used as an introductory guide, as you learn about the different features of Japanese food and cooking and the history and customs of its eating places. But, more importantly, it can be used as a handy reference book when you're in a restaurant, enabling you to read the menu and order on your own. So whether you're in downtown Tokyo or in some remote mountain village, you'll be able to walk into any restaurant you come across, with full confidence in your menu-reading abilities.

Features of *What's What in Japanese Restaurants*

"A Guide to Japanese Pronunciation" (page 21) will help you to correctly pronounce the names of dishes on the sample menus and the Japanese phrases for ordering.

"The Art of Japanese Cooking" (page 26) provides an introductory look at Japanese cooking and Japanese restaurants, and discusses their place in Japanese life.

"Restaurant Customs" (page 28) tells you what to expect when you walk into a restaurant, and explains the customs and practices that are different from those in Western restaurants.

"Phrases for Ordering in Japanese" (page 33) includes an extensive phrase section covering the most common restaurant situations, and some less common ones as well (such as making a reservation or ordering a vegetarian meal). Also included are possible waiter responses, so that after you ask a question you'll be able to understand the answer.

"Recognizing Specialty Restaurants" (page 40) explains how to find a restaurant and how to find out what kind of food it serves. You can recognize various specialty restaurants by comparing their signs with the illustrations in this chapter.

"Reading Numbers and Basic Vocabulary Terms" (page 45) covers menu terms common to many different types of restaurants (such as types of full-course meals, names of beverages, the Japanese characters used for numbers and prices, etc.), and can be used in conjunction with the sample specialty menus described below.

"Specialty Restaurants and Their Menus": individual restaurant chapters (pages 51–149).

Since most restaurants in Japan specialize in one particular cuisine or another, the second part of the book is divided into chapters corresponding to these different cuisines. Each chapter concentrates on one type of restaurant (such as sushi restaurants) and describes the food served there, covering some or all of the following information:

- Cooking methods and ingredients
- Descriptions of common dishes
- Regional variations
- Tips for ordering
- Sauces and condiments found on the table
- History of the cuisine
- Atmosphere of this type of restaurant
- Criteria for determining the best restaurants.

Following the text is a comprehensive sample menu, in Japanese and English, that closely approximates a real menu for the type of restaurant under discussion. Each item on the menu represents a popular dish, described as follows:

- Name of the dish in Japanese characters
- Transliteration into the Roman alphabet
- Translation
- Description of the dish and ingredients used.

Following the menu may be a short list of vocabulary words and useful phrases for the category of restaurant under discussion.

The text section of each restaurant chapter can be read on its own, and you may enjoy dipping into the various chapters at random and discovering specialty cuisines you may want to try later. The sample menu section is most useful when you're actually sitting at a table ordering, so don't forget to bring the book with you when you go out to eat.

"Boxed Lunches and Food Delivery" (page 150) describes Japanese boxed lunches (*bentō*) and department-store food floors, and also provides a how-to guide for getting food delivered from restaurants to your home.

"Drinking in Japan" (page 154) explains how and where to order a cocktail, going on to discuss some Japanese customs associated with drinking.

The **"Japanese Food Vocabulary and Glossary"** (page 161) provides an extensive list of food terms, with Japanese characters, transliterations, and English translations. This section may be most useful when buying food at the grocery store, or when trying to read the list of ingredients in the description of a dish on the menu.

The **"Hiragana and Katakana Charts"** (inside front and back covers) are a handy reference to the two Japanese syllabic writing systems. The *katakana* chart will be most useful when trying to figure out "Japanized" readings of foreign words. This is especially helpful when ordering in coffee shops, Western-style restaurants, and bars. Throughout the book, menus are given in Japanese characters, *hiragana*, and *katakana*, depending upon which style is most popular for that particular word.

How to Use This Book

Here are a few suggestions on the most effective ways to use this book, depending on your interests and the length of your stay in Japan.

1. *The quick and easy approach: Ordering directly from the sample menus*

If you're on a busy traveling schedule, the simplest approach may be to first turn to the appropriate sample menu in this book, find a dish that sounds interesting, and then see if they serve it. The most important step is to first find the right menu for the restaurant you're in, so consult **"Recognizing Specialty Restaurants"** on page 40 before you walk in. Just match the sign on the shop with the illustrations in the book. (If you can't figure out the sign, you can also walk in and ask what kind of food they serve; *see* page 45.)

Next, turn to the corresponding sample menu in the book, point to something you'd like to try, and ask if they have it by saying something like: "*Sumimasen ga, kore ga arimasu ka?*" (*see* page 21 for advice on correct pronunciation). If they say yes, ask them to bring you whatever you ordered. If they say no, then try again with another item. Most of the sample menus are arranged with the most commonly served items near the top. The "quick and easy" method of ordering may be difficult in the pub-style restaurants called *izakaya*, as well as in Chinese restaurants, which tend to have large and varied menus, but it should work fairly well in most other places.

2. *The methodical approach: Reading the actual menu*

If you want to figure out what the menu actually says, simply match up the Japanese characters on the real menu with the same characters on the sample menu, and then read across the sample menu to find the pronunciation and description of the dish. (As in the first approach, you must first determine what type of restaurant you're in by referring to page 40.) Point to what you want on the real menu, or use the phrases on page 33 to impress the waiter with your linguistic ability.

3. *The scholarly approach*

If you're going to be in Japan for an extended period of time, and especially if you're going to be studying Japanese reading and writing, you might want to study menu characters as well. You can use the same methods that you use for your regular studies, but you'll be able to apply the results more quickly. You'll also be able to dazzle your friends and acquaintances with your progress every time you go to a restaurant together.

A Guide to Japanese Pronunciation

Syllables

In spoken Japanese, each syllable is enunciated for approximately the same length of time. Long vowel sounds in Japanese are treated as extra syllables, so their duration should be twice as long as that of short vowels. Unlike in English, a stressed syllable in Japanese is indicated by a rise or fall in pitch, rather than by extended duration.

Vowels

Short vowels are pronounced much as in Italian; you should try to pronounce them as indicated below:

a	as in f<u>a</u>ther
e	as in g<u>e</u>t
i	as in macaron<u>i</u>
o	as in p<u>o</u>lo
u	as in p<u>u</u>t or b<u>oo</u>k

Long vowels should be pronounced for at least twice as long as short vowels. This is very important for comprehension, since very often two words will differ only in the length of the vowel. For example, the word *bīru*, with a long **ī**, means beer, while *biru*, with a short **i**, means building.

ā   as in dr<u>a</u>ma or <u>ah</u>
ē   as in Ma<u>y</u>
ī   as in kn<u>ee</u>
ō   as in <u>ow</u>n
ū   as in c<u>oo</u>l

Consonants

● Single Consonants
Most single consonants are pronounced as in English, with the following exceptions:

f(u)   The Japanese **f** only occurs in the syllable **fu**, and it is similar to the sound at the beginning of the word h<u>oo</u>p, but it should be pronounced while expelling air between the lips.

g   At the beginning of a word, this is always a hard **g**, as in gift, and never a soft **g**, as in gerbil. In the middle of a word it can be pronounced either as a hard **g**, or like the **ng** sound in the phrase "si<u>ng</u> a song"; either form can be understood.

n   There are two different **n** sounds in Japanese. The first occurs at the beginning of a syllable (e.g., as in *banira*, or vanilla); this is pronounced as in English. The second **n** sound is a syllabic **n**, and it occurs at the end of a word, before a consonant, or before a vowel (in this text a syllabic **n** before a vowel is indicated by an apostrophe: **n'**). (Examples of a syllabic **n** are *pan*, meaning bread, *anzu*, meaning apricot, and *kin'iro*, meaning gold color.)

The syllabic **n** is pronounced similarly to a French nasal **n**. When it occurs before a **b**, **m**, or **p**, the syllabic **n** sounds more like an **m**. (For example, the **m** sound in the word tempura is a syllabic **n**, and the word is actually spelled *tenpura* in strictly transliterated Japanese.)

r   The Japanese **r** is midway between the English **r** and **l** sounds, and it sometimes sounds almost like a **d**. It should be pronounced by touching the tongue to the ridge behind the upper teeth.

ts(u)   This is pronounced as in the phrase, "It's oolong tea."

● Double Consonants
A double consonant, pronounced much as in Italian (e.g., *hokke*, or mackerel, or *matcha*, or powdered green tea), is indicated by a syllable-length pause in speech before pronouncing the following consonant. We often do the same thing in English without being aware of it, as in the phrase, "It's hot today," in which the final **t** in "hot" is not fully pronounced but is indicated by a short pause, during which the tongue is held in the position of pronouncing that sound. Note that a short vowel before a double consonant should be pronounced normally, not as a long vowel.

● Consonant Followed by a **Y**
A consonant followed by a **y** and then by a vowel (as in *gyūniku*, or beef) is pronounced as one syllable. (In this case, the **y** is considered a consonant and is not pronounced as a vowel; thus, **yū** is pronounced as in the English "use.") For example, the word *gyōza* (Chinese–style dumpling) is pronounced GYO-O-ZA, not as GI-YO-O-ZA.

Unstressed Syllables

Certain syllables, such as **su**, are sometimes not fully voiced when they occur at the end of a word. Thus, the expression "*Aite imasu ka?*" ("Are you open?") is pronounced "A-I-TE I-MA-S' KA?"

PART I

About Japanese
Restaurants

The Art of Japanese Cooking

Specialty Cuisines

Visitors to Japan are often surprised that there are so many different styles of Japanese cooking. In Western countries, even the most devoted fans are usually exposed to only a handful of popular Japanese dishes: chicken teriyaki, beef sukiyaki, tempura, and sushi. But within Japan there are at least fifteen to twenty different cooking styles or cuisines, each style with its own contingent of specialty restaurants.

Regional geographical variations are responsible for some of this diversity. Japan is very mountainous, and until recently travel between the different parts of the country was difficult. As a result, different regions have developed their own individual cooking styles, based on local climate and locally available ingredients. Even today, in spite of improved transportation and a more mobile society, food preparation in the different sections of Japan is surprisingly varied. To give a single example: Visitors to Osaka who order sushi will find that it's made by pressing vinegared fish and cooked rice into special square molds, resulting in a dish quite different from the more familiar Tokyo variety.

In large metropolitan areas like Tokyo, you can find many regional restaurants that specialize in the cuisines of far-off corners of the country. Other specialty restaurants can be distinguished by a particular method of cooking. An example of this is restaurants that specialize in tempura, which may serve dozens of different kinds of delicacies, all lightly battered and deep-fried, tempura-style. Still other restaurants will specialize in only one particular type of food. For example, tofu (bean curd) restaurants serve every imaginable variation of tofu-based dishes, from tofu pudding and soy milk to deep-fried tofu "pouches" stuffed with delectable fillings; spicy tofu lasagna; and even tofu steaks.

A major reason for specialization is the intense degree of competition among eating places. With restaurants literally stacked one on top of another, a new restaurant that wants to carve a niche for itself will find it much easier to concentrate on one particular cuisine, rather than to try to cook every kind of food equally well.

Ingredients

Individual ingredients receive far more emphasis in Japanese cooking than in Western cuisine. Many cooking methods, such as tempura-style frying or *yakitori*-style charcoal grilling, are designed to capture the distinctive character and taste of one particular food at a time. Even Japanese stews and casseroles with many ingredients manage to offer the palate a succession of distinct flavors and textures rather than a blending of tastes.

This enhanced "visibility" of ingredients leads to a greater concern for both freshness and seasonality. Seasonal changes in particular are an important element of Japanese culture (and they are also strongly reflected in Japanese art and literature). Two ingredients especially dependent on the seasons are fresh vegetables and seafood, so it's not surprising to see sushi and tempura restaurants varying their offerings month by month. But even prepared foods such as Japanese sweets and Japanese pickles (each of which comes in many dozens of varieties) reflect changes of season, and completely different varieties are served at different times of the year. Some entire cuisines are seasonal as well; for example, *oden* (fishcake stews), *nabemono* (meat and fish stews), and *fugu* (blowfish dishes) are usually only served in the wintertime.

Since Japan is an island nation, fish and seafood are much more important than meat in traditional cooking. Fish appears in many unusual forms, including a wide variety of processed fish cakes used in soups, stews, and lunch boxes. Seaweed is also widely used, appearing most often as the thin, black, toasted sheets of *nori* seaweed that are used to wrap certain kinds of sushi. Rice, of course, is the most important staple food (in fact, one Japanese word for "meal" is the same as the word for rice), and pounded glutinous rice (called *mochi*) is an important ingredient in traditional desserts.

Visual Presentation

In Japanese cuisine, the presentation of food is every bit as important as the way it tastes. In fact, ingredients are often chosen specifically for their color, shape, or texture rather than their flavor. An example is *san-shoku* (three-colored) *soba*, a dish containing three different colors of buckwheat noodles (brown, white, and green) arranged harmoniously on a lacquer tray. Many other three-colored dishes can also be found, including a popular mixture of purple, white, and green Japanese pickles. Corner grocery stores even sell three-colored "mixed sand-wiches" with different-colored fillings.

Shape is also important, and a great deal of attention is paid to slic-ing and arranging foods. Attention to shape and color also extends to plates and bowls, which can be chosen to complement and highlight the food they hold. For example, round foods are often served on square dishes, and vice versa. Many traditional restaurants (and many private homes as well) also have different plates for each season of the year.

Kaiseki restaurants, which are very traditional (and also very expen-sive), go to the greatest lengths to make each meal an artistic event, paying infinite attention to every detail of its presentation (balance of color, texture, season, cooking method, and so forth). But even or-dinary restaurants make it a point to serve their food artistically, and they treat visual presentation as an intrinsic element of Japanese cuisine.

Restaurant Customs

Choosing a Restaurant

Since most Japanese restaurants specialize in a particular cuisine (such as sushi or tempura or grilled chicken), the first step in sizing up a restaurant is to figure out what their specialty is. This is usually written (in Japanese) somewhere on the shop sign or curtain. You can match the Japanese characters on the sign with the ones listed in the section **"Recognizing Specialty Restaurants"** (page 40), but there are often visual clues as well. For example, a picture of a pig might advertise a *tonkatsu* (pork cutlet) restaurant, and a stylized drawing of an eel would generally indicate a grilled-eel restaurant. And of course many restaurants display lifelike plastic models of the dishes they serve.

These models appear in the front window, along with the prices, to give passersby an idea of what to expect inside.

Hours of Service

Lunchtime in Japanese restaurants is usually from 11:30 AM or noon until 2 PM, and most places feature relatively inexpensive lunch specials. Workers in Japanese companies almost always take their lunch between twelve and one, so restaurants are jam-packed by 12:05 or so. The best time to get a seat is before 11:45 AM or after 1 PM. After 2 PM many places close for a few hours until dinner. However, restaurants in shopping districts, especially those inside department stores, are more likely to stay open throughout the day to accommodate those shoppers hungry for an afternoon snack.

In the evenings most restaurants outside of major shopping and entertainment districts close relatively early, often by 8 or 9 PM. In any neighborhood, finding a place to eat after 10 PM can be a bit difficult, and eating a meal after midnight may involve elaborate planning.

Most smaller restaurants are closed one day a week to give the staff a holiday. In business and residential neighborhoods the day off is usually (but not always) Sunday. If you're planning to go out of your way to a favorite restaurant, especially if you're planning to meet people there, it might be a good idea to telephone ahead of time. Almost all restaurants are closed for New Year's holidays during the first three or four days of January, and some are also closed for several days around the middle of August for the yearly *Obon* (All Souls') festival.

What to Expect Inside

Traditional Japanese restaurants usually hang a distinctive *noren*, or half-curtain, over the entrance, announcing the name of the shop and the type of cuisine served. The *noren* also indicates that the restaurant is open for business. (When the *noren* isn't over the door, it means the restaurant is closed.) Other shops use the sign (営業中) (*eigyōchū*, "open for business") to show they are open, and (準備中) (*junbichū*, literally "under preparation") to indicate that they are closed.

When you walk in you'll be greeted with a hearty welcome ("*Irasshaimase*") if the shop is open for business. After you're seated, you'll usually receive an *oshibori*, which is a hot, damp cloth towel (cold in the summer) to wipe your hands with. In sushi restaurants and drinking establishments the *oshibori* may also be used to wipe your fingers with during the meal; in other places the waiter will take it away immediately. By the way, many inexpensive restaurants don't provide napkins, although you can usually ask for a tissue in an emergency. Japanese people always carry a handkerchief wherever they go, and you may find it convenient to adopt this practice when in Japan.

There are a few Japanese restaurant customs that differ from those of Western restaurants. For example, when two people are eating together, they often order the same meal. Your waiter may ask if you want two of something (*"Futatsu desu ka?"*); if you want just one, answer "One, please" (*"Hitotsu kudasai"*), or simply hold up one finger.

Small restaurants in Japan tend to have very small kitchens, so if you're with several people, not everyone's food will be brought at the same time. This is one situation where everyday etiquette may give way to practical considerations, and the first person served may wish to begin eating while his food is still hot, rather than wait. When the food finally does come, the waiter or waitress will usually announce the name of each dish and ask who ordered it. Another point: If you happen to be drinking saké, the waiter will often bring only the appetizers until you're finished drinking. One reason for this is that saké is a kind of wine made of fermented rice, and it's traditionally never served at the same time as rice; another reason is that Japanese dining etiquette clearly separates the time set aside for enjoying a few drinks from the time devoted to enjoying one's meal.

Using Chopsticks

Flat, disposable wooden chopsticks (called *waribashi*) are the most common chopsticks in Japan. These are taken out of their wrapper and pulled apart before being used. Chopsticks are held at their thick end, with their tips evenly aligned. One stick is held stationary between the crook of the thumb and the tip of the ring finger. The other stick is grasped between the tip of the thumb and the tips of the index and middle fingers (in much the same way that you would hold a pencil, but closer to the thick end than to the point), and this stick is manipulated back and forth when picking up food.

What to Order

Although items on the menu can be ordered a la carte, many restaurants take this quite literally and serve you exactly what you ordered and nothing more; bread, rice, vegetables, pickles, soup, salad, and so forth must all be ordered separately. Most menus also list a variety of table d'hôte sets and combinations, and these are more economical than ordering a la carte. The simplest and most common set is the *teishoku*, or set meal, which includes the main dish, plus rice, soup, and a dish of pickles. **Lunch specials**, which usually have names like "A lunch" or "B lunch," are similar to *teishoku*, or they may include salad, a choice of bread or rice, and coffee, especially in Western-style restaurants.

"**Dinner sets**" in Japanese restaurants often include two or three different types of Japanese food, while in Western-style restaurants dinner sets usually include a main dish plus soup, bread, coffee or tea, and sometimes dessert. "**Course meals**" (again with names like "A course" and "B course") tend to be even more elaborate than dinner sets, and may include quite a number of different courses. In pub-type restaurants, the food is always served a la carte, and a meal can be made up of a number of small "side dishes." In some of the more down-to-earth places there is no menu at all, and the dishes available are listed on elaborately written strips of paper tacked up on the walls.

Ordering Drinks

When you order drinks, some restaurants and bars (especially those with "atmosphere") will bring you a small side dish, known as an *otōshi*, with your first round of drinks, and add the price to your bill. The *otōshi* can be anything from a tiny dish of peanuts to a tiny dish of pickled vegetables. It's usually inexpensive (anywhere from ¥100 to ¥500, depending on the style of the restaurant), and one is brought for each person drinking.

On the subject of drinking, beer is the most commonly served alcoholic beverage, and it's available at almost every restaurant (as well as in train stations, sidewalk vending machines, and many other unexpected places). Saké is often served at Japanese restaurants as well. Western-style restaurants usually serve some kind of wine, but regular mixed drinks and cocktails are much more difficult to find. (See "**Drinking in Japan**" on page 154 for more specific information.)

Paying the Check

If you're dining near the restaurant's closing time, often the waiter will come by your table to inform you that the kitchen is closing. He'll ask if you have any last orders for food or drink, using the Japanese term for "last order" (*rasuto ōdā*). Usually the check is left on your table after all your food has been brought. (This also gives you a chance to inform your waiter in case he's forgotten something). When you've finished eating, you may bring the bill up to the front register and pay there. (A few inexpensive restaurants use a ticket system, where you pay at the counter when you walk in, and you receive food tickets to give to your waiter.)

When the total food charge is over a certain amount (currently ¥7,000 per person), there is a special meal tax of 10% on top of the usual consumption tax (which is currently 3%). In addition to the food charges and the tax, there may occasionally be other items on the bill, according to the policies of the restaurant. These may include a 10% service charge (usually indicated on the menu), a table charge, a music charge (if there was entertainment), and the price of your *otōshi* appetizers if you've ordered drinks. There is no tipping in restaurants in Japan.

Etiquette and Ambience

As in other areas of Japanese life, there are many customs and rules of etiquette for eating in restaurants. Don't worry too much about these, though, since non-Japanese people aren't expected to know all the rules. Ordinary polite behavior and Western manners are quite sufficient for almost every situation. If you're in doubt about specific matters (such as which dish to use for your soy sauce), you can simply follow the example of your neighbors.

And whether you're in a raucous after-work pub serving *yakitori* or a subdued traditional *kaiseki* house, remember that Japanese restaurants are there primarily for the enjoyment of your food and the company of your dining companions. Most restaurants not only specialize in a particular cuisine, they also take a great deal of pride in the way they prepare and serve it. Polite service is the general rule, but many proprietors of smaller restaurants go even further and try to create a friendly and very personal atmosphere in their shops. So sit back, relax, and enjoy the food.

Phrases for Ordering in Japanese

Preliminaries

Are you open?　*Aite imasu ka?*　開いていますか?

Excuse me, what kind of food do you serve?
　　Sumimasen ga, donna ryōri ga arimasu ka?
　　すみませんが、どんな料理がありますか?

How long is the wait?
　　Dono kurai machimasu ka?　どのくらい待ちますか?

Can I sit at a table (not at the counter)?
　　(Kauntā denaku) tēburu ni suwaremasu ka?
　　(カウンターでなく)テーブルに座れますか?

Can we sit at that table? (pointing)
　　Ano tēburu de ii desu ka?　あのテーブルでいいですか?

Please bring the menu.
　　Menyū o onegai shimasu.　メニューをお願いします。

Please bring a glass of water.　*Mizu o kudasai.*　水をください。

Please bring water for everyone.
　　Minna ni mizu o kudasai.　みんなに水をください。

Do you take (credit cards/American Express/Visa)?
　　(Kurejitto kādo/Amerikan Ekusupuresu/Biza) wa tsukaemasu ka?
　　(クレジットカード/アメリカンエクスプレス/ビザ)は使えますか。

Can we get a children's high chair?
　　Kodomo-yō no isu wa arimasu ka?　子供用の椅子はありますか?

Please come back in a minute, (we're not ready to order yet).
　　Chotto matte kudasai, (mada ōdā ga kimatte imasen).
　　ちょっと待ってください、(まだオーダーが決まっていません)。

Ordering

Waiter. (Lit. ''Excuse me.'')　*Sumimasen.*　すみません。

Do you have this? (pointing to name of dish in this book)
  Kore arimasu ka? これありますか?

Do you have XX? *XX arimasu ka?* XX ありますか?

What do you recommend (today)?
  (Kyō no) osusume wa nan desu ka?
  (今日の)おすすめは何ですか?

Can we have the selections of the chef? (sushi restaurants)
  Tekitō ni mitsukurotte kudasai. 適当に見繕ってください。

I'll have (this/that).
  (Kore/Are) o kudasai. (これ/あれ)をください。

I'll have XX. *XX o kudasai.* XX をください。

In addition, I'll have YY.
  Sore kara, YY o kudasai. それから、YY をください。

How much is (this/that).
  (Kore/Are) wa ikura desu ka? (これ/あれ)はいくらですか?

I'll have the XX *teishoku* (table d'hôte).
  XX teishoku o kudasai. XX 定食をください。

I'll have XX a la carte.
  XX o ippin de kudasai. XX を一品でください。

I'll have the "A course." *"Ē kōsu" o kudasai.* A コースをください。

I'll have the "B lunch," with bread.
  "Bī ranchi" ni pan o kudasai. B ランチにパンをください。

We'll have (one/two) beer(s).
  Bīru o (hitotsu/futatsu) kudasai. ビールを(一つ/二つ)ください。

Do you have any wine? *Wain wa arimasu ka?* ワインはありますか?

I'll have a (glass/bottle) of (red wine/white wine).
  (Gurasu/Botoru) de (aka wain/shiro wain) o kudasai.
  (グラス/ボトル)で(赤ワイン/白ワイン)をください。

Cancel the XX. *XX o torikeshite kudasai.* XX を取り消してください。

I'll have XX instead of YY.
  YY no kawari ni XX o kudasai. YY のかわりに XX をください。

What is that person eating? (pointing to another table)
  Ano hito ga tabete iru no wa nan desu ka?
  あの人が食べているのは何ですか?

I ordered that. (Lit. "Over here.")
Kochira desu.　こちらです。

(He/she) ordered that. (pointing)
(Kare/Kanojo) desu.　（彼/彼女）です。

Is (coffee/XX) included with the meal?
(Kōhī/XX) ga tsuite imasu ka?
（コーヒー/**XX**）がついていますか？

I'll have the coffee (right away/after the meal).
Kōhī wa (ima/shokugo ni) kudasai.
コーヒーは（今/食後に）ください。

Yes.　*Hai.*　はい。

No.　*Iie.*　いいえ。

No more, thank you.　*Mō kekkō desu, dōmo.*　もう結構です，どうも。

Just a little.　*Sukoshi dake kudasai.*　少しだけください。

A second helping of (this/rice), please.
(Kore/raisu) no okawari o kudasai.
（これ/ライス）のおかわりをください。

Special Orders

Do you have any vegetarian dishes (without meat or fish)?
Niku mo sakana mo haitte inai ryōri ga arimasu ka?
肉も魚も入っていない料理がありますか？

I can't eat (meat/pork/beef).
Watashi wa (niku/pōku/bīfu) ga taberaremasen.
私は（肉/ポーク/ビーフ）が食べられません。

I can't eat (seafood/sugar).
Watashi wa (shīfūdo/satō) ga taberaremasen.
私は（シーフード/砂糖）が食べられません。

Does (this/that) have sugar?
(Kore/Are) ni wa satō ga haitte imasu ka?
（これ/あれ）には砂糖が入っていますか？

Can I have (that/XX) without (sugar/salt/meat/ice)?
(Satō/Shio/Niku/Kōri) nashi de (are/XX) o kudasai.
（砂糖/塩/肉/氷）なしで（あれ/**XX**）をください。

Other Requests

Excuse me, where's the bathroom?
Sumimasen, toire wa doko desu ka?
すみません，トイレはどこですか?

Do you have a telephone?
Sumimasen, denwa wa arimasu ka?
すみません，電話はありますか?

Could you please cook (this/the bacon/the XX) more?
(Kore/Bēkon/XX) o motto yoku yaite kudasai.
(これ/ベーコン/XX)をもっとよく焼いてください。

Could you please wrap this up to go?
Kore o tsutsunde kuremasen ka?　これを包んでくれませんか?

Could I please have a (napkin/knife and fork/spoon/pair of chopsticks)?
(Nafukin/Naifu to fōku/Supūn/Hashi) o kudasai.
(ナフキン/ナイフとフォーク/スプーン/箸)をください。

Can we please have another (two plates/glass)?
Mō (futatsu sara/hitotsu koppu) o kudasai.
もう(二つ，皿/一つ，コップ)をください。

What do you have for dessert?
Dezāto wa nani ga arimasu ka?　デザートは何がありますか?

Do you have any toothpicks?　*Yōji o kudasai.*　楊枝をください。

Services and Hours

Can I order something to take out?
Nani ka mochikaeri ni dekimasu ka?
何か持ち帰りにできますか?

Do you deliver as far as XX?
XX made demae dekimasu ka?　XX まで出前できますか?

Do you have a delivery menu?
Demae no menyū wa arimasu ka?　出前のメニューはありますか?

What time is the last order?
Rasuto ōdā wa nanji desu ka?　ラストオーダーは何時ですか?

What day are you closed?
Oyasumi wa itsu desu ka?　お休みはいつですか?

Can I have a (matchbook/map)?
Omise no (matchi/chizu) wa arimasu ka?
お店の（マッチ/地図）はありますか?

Paying

Could we please have the check?
Okanjō o onegai shimasu. お勘定をお願いします。

Would you please show me the check?
Denpyō o misete kudasai. 伝票を見せてください。

How much is it? *Ikura desu ka?* いくらですか?

Could we please pay separately? (at register)
Betsu-betsu ni onegai shimasu. 別々にお願いします。

I had the XX and the YY.
Watashi wa XX to YY o haraimasu. 私は XX と YY を払います。

Can I please have change for this?
Kore o kuzushite kudasai. これをくずしてください。

Thanks for the great meal. (said to host and/or restaurant staff)
Gochisō sama deshita. ごちそうさまでした。

Please give me a receipt.
Ryōshūsho o onegai shimasu. 領収書をお願いします。

Thank you. *Dōmo arigatō.* どうもありがとう。

It was delicious. *Oishikatta desu.* おいしかったです。

On the Telephone

Are you open today?
Kyō wa eigyō shite imasu ka? 今日は営業していますか?

Can I make reservations for tonight?
Konban, yoyaku wa dekimasu ka? 今晩，予約はできますか?

I'd like a table for (two persons/four persons) at (7:30/8:00).
(Shichi-ji han/Hachi-ji) ni (futari/yonin) no yoyaku o shitai no desu ga...
（七時半/八時）に（二人/四人）の予約をしたいのですが…

My name is XX.
Watashi no namae wa XX desu. 私の名前は XX です。

Numbers

	General items		Bottles of beer or sticks of yakitori	
one	hitotsu	一つ	i-ppon	一本
two	futatsu	二つ	ni-hon	二本
three	mittsu	三つ	san-bon	三本
four	yottsu	四つ	yon-hon	四本
five	itsutsu	五つ	go-hon	五本
six	muttsu	六つ	ro-ppon	六本
seven	nanatsu	七つ	nana-hon	七本

Waiter Responses

Welcome.　*Irasshaimase.*　いらっしゃいませ。

Sorry, we're closed.
(Sumimasen,) heiten desu./mō owari desu.
(すみません、)閉店です。/もう終わりです。

There's a (momentary/twenty-minute) wait.
(Shōshō/Nijuppun gurai) omachi kudasai.
(少々/二十分位)おまちください。

Do you mind sitting at the counter?
Kauntā de yoroshii desu ka?
カウンターでよろしいですか?

Do you mind sharing a table?
Aiseki de yoroshii desu ka?
あい席でよろしいですか?

Are you ready to order?
(Ōdā/Gochūmon) wa (kimari mashita/yoroshii desu) ka?
(オーダー/ご注文)は(決まりました/よろしいです)か?

What would you like?　*Nani ni nasaimasu ka?*　何になさいますか?

Yes.　*Hai/Sō desu.*　はい/そうです。

No.　*Iie/Nai desu/Chotto nai desu.*
いいえ/ないです/ちょっとないです。

Sorry, we're out of that.
Sumimasen, sore wa kirashite imasu.
すみません，それは切らしています。

We don't have that.
(Sore wa) oite imasen/nai desu.
（それは）置いていません／ないです。

We can't do that.　　*Sore wa dekimasen.*　それはできません。

Do you want an extra-large portion?
Ōmori ni shimasu ka?　大盛りにしますか？

Do you want that as a *teishoku* (set meal with rice and soup)?
Sore o (teishoku/setto) ni shimasu ka?
それを（定食／セット）にしますか？

What would you like to drink?　　*Onomimono wa?*　お飲み物は……？

Do you want your coffee hot or iced?
Kōhī wa hotto to aisu, dochira ni shimasu ka?
コーヒーはホットとアイスどちらにしますか？

Do you want your coffee now or at the end of the meal?
Kōhī wa (ima/shokugo/itsu) ni shimasu ka?
コーヒーは（今／食後／いつ）にしますか？

Do you want bread or rice?
Pan to raisu, dochira ni shimasu ka?
パンとライス，どちらにしますか？

That's included with your meal.
Sore wa tsuite imasu.　それはついています。

Wait a moment, please.
(Shōshō/Sukoshi) omachi kudasai.　（少々／少し）お待ちください。

Sorry to have kept you waiting.
Omatase shimashita.　お待たせしました。

Who ordered the XX?　　*XX wa dochira desu ka?*　XX はどちらですか？

This is the last order, the kitchen is closing.
Rasuto ōdā desu ga, (gochūmon wa arimasu ka?)
ラストオーダーですが，（ご注文はありますか？）

May I take your plates?
(Sara o) osage shite yoroshii desu ka?
（皿を）お下げしてよろしいですか？

Please come again. *Mata okoshi kudasai.* またお越しください。

Reservations aren't necessary.
Yoyaku wa hitsuyō arimasen. 予約は必要ありません。

What time? *Nanji ni itashimasu ka?* 何時にいたしますか?

How many people? *Nan-mei-sama desu ka?* 何名様ですか?

What's your name?
Onamae o itadakemasu ka? お名前をいただけますか?

⚜
Recognizing Specialty Restaurants

Finding a Restaurant

If you've just spent a long day sightseeing or shopping (or even work-ing), and you're starting to get hungry, you may be wondering how to find a decent restaurant as quickly as possible. Depending on where you are, there are certain places to look that will help speed up your search. If you're in a shopping neighborhood, for example, one of the best places to look is on top of department stores. Usually there'll be a restaurant floor (or floors) at the very top, with a variety of different types of restaurants, each with a display window filled with plastic models of the food inside. Restaurants in department stores tend to be moderately priced and clean, and you can easily wander from window to window looking for something that strikes your fancy. Food floors stay open a few hours later than the closing time of the department store (generally until 9 or 10 PM), so if the store itself is closed, look for the special elevators that go to the top. In business districts, often large office buildings will have similar restaurant floors in their basements. Some skyscrapers also have top-floor restaurants with panoramic views.

In other neighborhoods, restaurants tend to be easiest to find in the vicinity of train stations. There are also narrow streets and alleys called *shōtengai* (shopping arcades), often leading away from stations. These are lively little streets lined with all sorts of stores—vegetable stands, *tàtami* (grass mat) weavers, tofu makers, and many small restaurants.

If you're looking for someplace special or exotic (the best tofu restaurant in Osaka, for example), most travel guidebooks have restaurant listings. (One book I especially like is *Gateway to Japan* by June Kinoshita and Nicholas Palevsky [Kodansha International, 1992].) It should be noted, though, that finding a specific location in Japan can be rather difficult—the system of addresses is quite complicated to the Western mind, and since most streets are unnamed, street directions rely a lot on "landmarks" ("turn left at the alley just past the big green building"). If you do get lost, you can show the address to a local policeman; they seem to have figured out the address system, and they're often helpful when approached. If you happen to find an interesting restaurant on your own, try to get a matchbook or store card with a map, so you can find it again or recommend it to your friends.

Recognizing Restaurants

Since the majority of restaurants in Japan specialize in a particular method of cooking, the menus in this book are organized in the same way, to reflect the actual restaurant menus you're likely to come across. The chart at the end of this section will help you recognize the various specialty restaurants.

Specialty restaurants almost always indicate the type of cuisine somewhere on their sign or *noren* (entrance curtain). The chart below lists the specialty restaurants covered in this book, and shows the Japanese characters to look out for. If you can't match up the characters immediately, there may sometimes be other visual clues, such as a small red lantern for a *yakitori* or *robatayaki* restaurant or an *izakaya*, or a picture of a cow for a *teppanyaki* or sukiyaki restaurant; these are also listed in the chart below. Note that these visual indicators are not necessarily consistent from one restaurant to the next; they are listed simply as general guidelines.

Another important clue is the plastic food models in the display window; for example, if all the dishes feature noodles, then the restaurant probably specializes in either *soba*, *udon*, or *rāmen* noodle dishes. Although usually the plastic food models represent cooked dishes, in some cases, such as with *nabemono*-type stews, the display in the window will show a plate containing the raw ingredients.

If you can't determine the specialty cuisine of a restaurant you're interested in, it might not have a specialty. Certain restaurants serve a wider variety of foods. For example, there are traditional Japanese *wafū* restaurants, often found in department stores, that may serve sushi, tempura, *kamameshi*, and other dishes. There are also general-purpose pubs that serve drinks and a wide variety of side dishes, both Japanese and Western-style. In addition there are expensive, traditional *kaiseki* restaurants and places that serve regional specialties. These restaurants are more fully described in "**Nihon-ryōri (General Japanese Cuisine)**" on page 120, and some clues for recognizing them are included in the chart below.

In case you're completely stumped—for example, when the sign is in hard-to-read script and there are no plastic models in the window, you can always walk in and ask what kind of food they serve; usually restaurant personnel are very helpful and they'll either tell you or point to the appropriate part of this book to use.

Japanese Chars.	Type of Restaurant	Food Served (and Displayed in Window) [Visual and Other Clues]
すし/スシ/寿司/鮨	**Sushi** (p. 52)	fish and seafood on fingers of rice [polished light wood counters inside, glass refrigerated cases with fish]
うなぎ/鰻	**Unagi** (p. 61)	grilled eel [う character in shape of eel]
ふぐ/フグ/河豚	**Fugu** (p. 64)	blowfish [drawings or models of blowfish]
てんぷら/テンプラ/天ぷら/天婦羅	**Tempura** (p. 66)	deep-fried seafood, vegetables
そば/ソバ/蕎麦	**Soba** (p. 71)	noodles (buckwheat; thin, brown)
うどん/ウドン	**Udon** (p. 71)	noodles (wheat; thick, white)
とんかつ/トンカツ/豚カツ	**Tonkatsu** (p. 78)	deep-fried pork cutlet [drawing of pig]
くしあげ/串揚	**Kushiage** (p. 81)	deep-fried seafood, vegetables, on skewers

やきとり/ヤキトリ/ 焼とり/焼鳥	**Yakitori** (p. 84)	grilled chicken on skewers [small red lantern in front, with writing]
かまめし/釜めし/ 釜飯	**Kamameshi** (p. 89)	rice with various toppings [cast-iron kettle, bowls in window in square wooden frames]
なべ/ナベ/鍋(物)	**Nabemono** (p. 92)	hotpot stews (plates of raw in- gredients [large caldron on display]
すきやき/スキヤキ/ 好き焼/鋤焼	**Sukiyaki** (p. 96)	hotpot-style beef [drawing of cow]
しゃぶしゃぶ/ シャブシャブ	**Shabu-shabu** (p. 96)	hotpot-style beef [drawing of cow]
おでん/オデン	**Oden** (p. 99)	fish-cake stew
おこのみやき/ お好み焼	**Okonomiyaki** (p. 102)	savory pancakes, fried noodles [tables inside with built-in grills]
てっぱん焼/鉄板焼	**Teppanyaki** (p. 105)	grilled beef steaks [drawing of cow]
居酒屋	**Izakaya** (p. 107)	beer, various foods [large red lanterns, noisy at- mosphere, statues of badgers]
ろばた焼/炉端焼	**Robatayaki** (p. 114)	grilled fish and other foods [rustic appearance]
地方料理/郷土料理	**Regional country-style**	various Japanese dishes [rustic appearance, waterwheels, carved bears, etc.]
	(**Note:** *See* page 116 for names of various regions in Japan.)	
日本料理/和風	**Nihon-ryōri (Jap. style)** (p. 120)	sushi, tempura, *kamameshi*, other food [traditional appearance and music, variety of foods on display, often located in department stores]

会席/懐石 料亭 割烹	**Kaiseki, ryōtei, kappō** (p. 120)	traditional Japanese [expensive and discreet traditional appearance]
京風	**Kyoto-style** (p. 120)	various Japanese dishes [traditional, elegant appearance]
やきにく/焼肉	**Yakiniku** (p. 128)	grilled beef, Korean-style [drawing of cow, tables inside with built-in grills and overhead vents]
らーめん/ラーメン/ 拉麺/中華	**Rāmen** (p. 132)	noodles (wheat and eggs; rather yellowish)
中国/中華 台湾 北京	**Chinese**(p. 132) (Taiwan) (Peking)	various (including *rāmen*) [Chinese-style decor: red lacquer, gold trim, dragons, etc.]
ビアガーデン	**Beer garden** (p. 154)	beer, various foods [located on department store roofs]
コーヒー/珈琲/喫茶	**Coffee shops** (p. 145)	coffee, spaghetti, sandwiches, cakes, etc. [coffee cups or coffee beans displayed]
甘味(処)	**Jap. dessert** (p. 141)	Japanese tea, Japanese-style desserts [traditional appearance]

Other Restaurant Signs

豆腐料理	**Tofu**	フランス料理	**French**
かに料理	**Crab**	イタリア料理	**Italian**
牛丼	**Gyūdon** (fast-food- type beef over rice)	地中海料理	**Mediterranean**
		インド料理	**Indian**
営業中	**open**	レストラン街/ 味の名店街	**Restaurant Floor**
準備中	**closed for cleaning**		

(本日)休業 **closed today**	ショッピング街/	**Shopping Arcade**
/閉店	商店街	

Useful Phrases

Excuse me, what kind of food do you serve here?
Sumimasen ga, koko de wa nan no ryōri o taberaremasu ka?
すみませんが，ここでは何の料理を食べられますか？

Could you please point to it in this book?
Koko kara yubisashite oshiete kudasai.
ここから指差して教えてください。

❦

Reading Numbers and Basic Vocabulary Terms

This section will help you read Japanese numbers and certain basic menu terms such as "*teishoku*" (set meal). It should be used in conjunction with the specialty sample menus. Refer to the chapter "**Phrases for Ordering in Japanese**" for help in ordering, and the "**Introduction**" for guidance in using this book.

Prices

○	0	五	5		十	10
一	1	六	6		百	100
二	2	七	7		千	1,000
三	3	八	8		万	10,000
四	4	九	9		円	¥

値段 *nedan*—price

千二百八十円　or　一、二八〇円　or　千二百八十円　¥1,280

Set Meals

定食	teishoku	set meal (main dish plus rice, pickles, and soup)
ランチ	ranchi	lunch special (usually similar to teishoku)
A ランチ	"Ē" ranchi	"A" lunch special
コース	kōsu	"course meal" (usually larger than teishoku, sometimes with dessert and/or appetizer)
並	nami	regular (usually said of quality)
上	jō	special (usually said of quality)
特上	tokujō	deluxe (usually said of quality)
梅(定食)	ume (teishoku)	regular (lit. "plum") set
竹(定食)	take (teishoku)	special (lit. "bamboo") set
松(定食)	matsu (teishoku)	extra-special (lit. "pine") set
菊, 蘭, 花, 月, 雪	kiku, ran, hana, tsuki, yuki	These are all various kinds of super-deluxe sets. (Their names literally mean "chrysanthemum," "orchid," "flower," "moon," and "snow.")
子供セット	kodomo setto	children's set
お子様ランチ	o-kosama ranchi	children's lunch
レディースコース	redīsu kōsu	"ladies' course"
幕の内(弁当)	maku-no-uchi (bentō)	special of the house (in a lacquer box)
おこのみ/お好み	okonomi	"favorite" set
盛り合わせ	moriawase	assortment
おすすめ	osusume	special of the day

Parts of the Menu

スープ	sūpu	soup
前菜	zensai	appetizers

オードブル	*ōdoburu*	hors d'oeuvres
サラダ	*sarada*	salad
一品（料理）	*ippin (ryōri)*	a la carte dishes
おつまみ	*otsumami*	snack dishes
ごはんもの/御飯物	*gohan mono*	rice dishes
（お/御）食事	*(o)shokuji*	meals with rice
さしみ/刺身	*sashimi*	raw fish dishes
さかな/魚	*sakana*	fish dishes
すのもの/酢の物	*su no mono*	pickled dishes
やきもの/焼物	*yaki mono*	broiled dishes
くしやき/串焼	*kushi yaki*	skewered foods (see "**Yakitori**" and "**Kushiage**" menus)
あげもの/揚げ物	*age mono*	fried dishes
おまかせ	*omakase*	chef's suggestions
デザート	*dezāto*	desserts
（お/御）のみもの/飲み物	*(o)nomimono*	beverages
ドリンク	*dorinku*	beverages

Menu Notations and Vocabulary

一付	*-tsuki*	included
A または B/A 又は B	*Ē mata wa Bī*	A or B
パンまたはライス/パン又はライス	*pan mata wa raisu*	bread or rice
ふつう/普通	*futsū*	regular
XX 入り	*XX iri*	with XX added
10%飲食税	*10% inshoku zei*	10% restaurant tax
10%サービス料	*10% sābisu ryō*	10% service charge

Common Food and Beverage Terms

Note: Please refer also to the sections "**Drinking in Japan**" (page 154) and "**Coffee Shops**" (page 145) for other beverage names.

みそ汁/味噌汁	*miso-shiru*	soybean-paste (*miso*) soup

(お/御)しんこ/新香	*oshinko*	Japanese-style pickled vegetables
さしみ/刺身	*sashimi*	raw fish platter (see also "**Sushi Menu**")
ビール	*bīru*	beer
生ビール	*nama bīru*	draft beer
大	*ō/dai*	large size
中	*chū*	medium size
小	*shō/ko*	small size
ビールを一本 ください。	*Bīru o ippon kudasai.*	One bottle of beer, please.
ジュース	*jūsu*	fruit-flavored drink, but the word is used as a generic term that includes everything from fresh orange juice and artificially flavored melon "juice" to American-style carbonated beverages
ウイスキー	*uisukī*	whiskey
水割	*mizuwari*	whiskey and water
(お/御)さけ/酒	*(o)saké*	Japanese rice wine

Using the Sample Menus

The chapters in Part II contain sample menus that show the dishes available in the particular types of restaurant covered. A portion of a typical sample menu is shown below.

Japanese written forms	Transliteration into Roman letters	Description of dish
茶づけ/茶漬	*chazuke*	steamed white rice with various garnishes, over which hot green tea has been poured

48

Once you've found the appropriate chapter for the type of restaurant you're in (see "**Recognizing Specialty Restaurants**," page 40), you can use the sample menu given in that chapter in one of two ways.

The easier method is to find something that looks interesting or appealing on the sample menu, point to it, and ask if they have it: *Kore ga arimasu ka?*

The other method is to match the characters on the actual menu you are given with the Japanese written forms shown in the sample menu; then you can either point to it or ask for it by name, using the pronunciation guide on page 21. (See the "How to Use This Book" section of the "**Introduction**" for more advice on how to go about ordering.)

Japanese Writing on the Sample Menus

In the sample menus, many Japanese terms are shown in two different forms, the *kanji* form, based upon Chinese characters, and a *kana* form, utilizing one of the two 46-character Japanese phonetic alphabets.

On the actual Japanese menus you'll come across, the names of dishes may appear in either *kanji* or *kana* form (depending upon the whims of the menu writer). Therefore, if a dish you're interested in on the sample menu has two forms, check to see if either one of them appears on the real menu. Other Japanese words, especially those of foreign origin, have no *kanji* equivalent; these are shown only in *kana* on the sample menus.

There are two different *kana* alphabets. Words of foreign origin are generally written with the squarer-looking *kana* alphabet called *katakana*, while native Japanese words are often written in the more cursive *hiragana*. For your reference, these two alphabets are shown on the inside front and back covers, but you won't need them to use the sample menus. Just match the Japanese writing on the sample menu with the actual menu you receive in a restaurant; in that way, you'll be able to order exactly what you want (if they have it).

[**Note:** In a few instances, compound words such as *yakitori* (grilled chicken) may be written with one part of the word in *kanji* and the other part in *hiragana*. So *yakitori*, usually written (やきとり) in *hiragana*, or (焼鳥) in *kanji*, may occasionally be written using a combination of forms, such as (焼とり).]

Horizontal and Vertical Writing

The sample menus use the horizontal writing style (read from left to right, like English). Some actual menus will use a vertical writing style (read from top to bottom and from right to left). The major difference on menus is that in horizontal writing, a long horizontal dash (—) is used to represent a long vowel sound in a *katakana* word, while in vertical writing a long vertical dash (|) is used. Thus, the word for coffee, *kōhī*, is written as follows in the two different styles:

コ ー ヒ ー

コ
|
ヒ
|

[**Note:** In constructing the sample menus, I have tried to use the Japanese written forms that most commonly appear on real menus. On a few occasions the written form of a word on an actual menu may differ slightly from the form shown on the sample menu. Also, menu writers will occasionally decide to write a word using the *katakana* alphabet (shown on the inside back cover) rather than the more common *hiragana* form shown on the sample menu. In this case you may refer to the **Katakana Chart**, or simply ask the waiter if they have what you want.]

PART II

Specialty Restaurants and Their Menus

Sushi
すし・スシ・寿司・鮨

Sushi is perhaps Japan's best-known contribution to world cuisine. The choicest, tenderest morsels of fresh raw fish are artfully arranged on individual "fingers" of vinegared rice by a skilled chef, then placed on a gleaming cypress counter in front of the eagerly waiting customer a few seconds later. Absolute freshness of the fish is the all-important factor for good sushi. In fact, some devotees prefer their sushi as early in the day as possible, and make the early-morning trip to the mecca of the sushi world, Tsukiji Market (Tokyo's wholesale fish market). There, at six-thirty in the morning, surrounded by the hustle and bustle of the daily fish auction, sitting in tiny stalls, they can eat the absolute freshest of the day's catch.

Sushi Restaurants

Even if you don't make the trip to Tsukiji Market, you'll be able to find plenty of good sushi shops and memorable food. Busy sushi restaurants have a lively and noisy atmosphere—the chefs behind the counter are constantly shouting orders, greeting customers, slicing, arranging, and generally putting on a show for the patrons. The best place to sit is at the counter, where you can watch the chefs at work and enjoy the spirited give and take between chef and customer as you order your sushi by the piece.

Although sushi seems like a simple food (it's not even cooked, after all), sushi preparation is actually a highly developed discipline, requiring years of apprenticeship under a master chef. If you watch closely, you may notice some of the chef's special techniques, such as dipping his hands in cold vinegared water before handling the fish, which both keeps the fish cool and fresh and prevents germs from his hands from contaminating the fresh fish. Sushi chefs always work quickly when handling the seafood, to keep it from heating in their hands, and they rarely talk while they're actually preparing the sushi.

Ordering

Since eating sushi is regarded as a gourmet dining experience, sushi restaurants tend to be more expensive than average, and some of them are quite steep. Pricing is sometimes a bit arbitrary; many places don't post prices for individual items, since the selection and quality of the seafood are constantly changing. If possible, your best bet is to go to a restaurant accompanied by a friend who goes there often. Otherwise, if you're on a budget, you might want to sit at a table and order a set meal—it's less complicated than ordering by the piece, and you'll have a better idea of what it's going to cost.

If you're adventurous and sit at the counter, you should generally order individual items, either from the menu or by pointing to what you want in the glass refrigerator boxes along the counter. Be prepared not to be surprised, because you will be served two pieces of anything you ask for (except *temaki*). You can also ask for the "catch of the day" (see menu section).

If you sit at a table, the method of ordering will vary from shop to shop. Sometimes you can order by item, but in other places the waiter will ask for your favorites, then the chef will prepare an assortment featuring those items and other selections of the day. If that's too complicated, you can always order a set meal (such as a *jō nigiri moriawase*, or deluxe assortment plate), or ask for the fish of the day (see menu section).

Although there's a special sushi-shop lingo used by the staff at sushi shops, it's easier to use the ordinary Japanese words when asking for soy sauce or chopsticks or the like. (By analogy, if you were in a diner in New York you'd ask for "two fried eggs on toast," even though the waitress might shout "Adam and Eve on a raft" to the cook.) One special sushi term that you might run across, however, is *agari* ("completion"), which is the name for the green tea served at the end of the meal.

Sushi restaurants are run primarily for eating, rather than drinking, and good shops rely on a rapid turnover in order to offer a wide variety of the freshest catch. If you're sitting at a busy counter it's impolite to dawdle after you've finished eating, especially if people are waiting. In some places the waiter will keep bringing food to your table as long as you sit there, since he assumes that you want to keep eating. If you're full but not quite ready to leave you should tell them you've had enough food (see menu section below).

Types of Sushi

Nigiri-zushi is the best-known variety; it consists of a piece of fish or seafood placed on an oblong-shaped finger of lightly vinegared rice and seasoned with a dab of horseradish. The fish is generally raw; however, shellfish are sometimes cooked. When fish roe is used as the topping, the whole concoction is wrapped in dried seaweed to keep it together. *Nigiri-zushi* can be picked up either by hand or with chopsticks, and is dipped in soy sauce quickly to keep the rice from falling apart. (*Nigiri-zushi* is traditionally a Tokyo dish, and it's also known as *Edomae-zushi*, Edo being the pre-1868 name of Tokyo.)

Maki-zushi is made with a bamboo mat, which is used to form strips of tuna or cucumber and a mass of vinegared rice into long, seaweed-covered rolls. The rolls are then cut into slices. *Maki-zushi* is usually eaten with chopsticks.

Temaki is similar to *maki-zushi*, except that it's made by hand and the finished roll is cone-shaped. It's eaten by hand, with or without soy sauce.

Sashimi is an assortment of sliced raw fish served on a platter with shredded radish and other garnishes. It's often served as an appetizer with drinks.

Chirashi consists of *sashimi* and chopped vegetables arranged over a bowl of rice. It usually comes as a set meal, in various sizes.

Oshi-zushi is a specialty of Osaka, and it's made by pressing a layer of fish (highly vinegared and sometimes lightly steamed) over a layer of rice in a large wooden mold. Afterwards, the *oshi-zushi* is removed from the mold and cut into bite-sized rectangular pieces.

Inari-zushi consists of rice and chopped vegetables wrapped in a pouch of fried tofu, and it is sometimes served at non-sushi restaurants and outdoor food stalls.

The first three types of sushi can be ordered individually, or in various combinations and set meals. *Sashimi* and *chirashi* are ready-made assortments, available in different sizes and prices. *Oshi-zushi* is most often served in the Kansai region (around Kyoto and Osaka).

Eating

Pour a small amount of soy sauce into the smallest dish, and dip your sushi into it quickly. If you're extremely skillful with chopsticks, the preferred technique is to turn the sushi upside down as you dip, so that you season the topping rather than the rice. When eating *sashimi* or *chirashi*, you should first mix a little *wasabi* (green horseradish) into the soy sauce. Be careful not to eat the *wasabi* by itself, since it's quite strong.

Thinly sliced pickled ginger can be eaten between bites of fish in order to refresh the palate and to help you differentiate between the various tastes. Green tea is always served to complete the meal.

Conveyor-belt Sushi

Many kinds of restaurants have their fast-food counterparts, and sushi is no exception. Mostly located near train stations, conveyor-belt sushi restaurants feature oval-shaped counters with endless processions of sushi moving past on metal conveyor belts. Shiny metal taps above the counter provide scalding hot green tea. Usually there are one or two chefs in the middle, keeping the belt full of fresh sushi and taking special orders.

Although they don't provide quite the same atmosphere as regular restaurants, and the cuts of fish may not be as expensive, generally the fish and seafood are fresh, especially during busy times. You're also assured of fast service and very reasonable prices. And of course the problems of ordering disappear, since you just choose whatever you like as it parades past you on the conveyor belt.

The best time to go is when it's somewhat crowded, since that means the sushi hasn't been sitting on the conveyor belt for too long. Find an empty seat at the counter, pour yourself a cup of tea from the spigot, then grab anything that looks interesting as it passes by. Soy sauce, chopsticks, and sliced ginger are available right on the counter. As you eat, stack the empty plates in front of you; when you're all done they'll count your dishes and charge you accordingly. (Sometimes there's a price code depending on the color or pattern of the dishes, but even the most expensive dishes are still very cheap.) If you want something special that you don't see on the conveyor belt, you can ask the chef behind the counter to make it for you, but the selection tends to be more limited than at regular restaurants.

SUSHI MENU

Set Meals

すし/寿司/鮨	*sushi*	any variety of raw fish and rice dish
にぎり（鮨）	*nigiri(-zushi)*	pieces of raw fish over vinegared rice balls
江戸前鮨	*Edomae-zushi*	same as *nigiri-zushi*
ちらし鮨	*chirashi(-zushi)*	assorted raw fish and vegetables over rice
並–	*nami-*	regular
中–	*chū-*	same as *nami*
上–	*jō-*	deluxe
特上–	*tokujō-*	extra-deluxe
上ちらし	*jō-chirashi*	deluxe order of *chirashi-zushi*

Maki-zushi

巻もの	*maki-mono*	vinegared rice and fish (or other ingredients) rolled in *nori* seaweed
てっか巻/鉄火巻	*tekka-maki*	tuna-filled *maki-zushi*
かっぱ巻	*kappa-maki*	cucumber-filled *maki-zushi*
鉄かっぱ巻	*tekkappa-maki*	selection of both tuna and cucumber rolls
（お/御）しんこ巻/新香巻	*(o)shinko-maki*	pickled-*daikon* (radish) rolls
かいわれ巻	*kaiware-maki*	*daikon*-sprout roll
うめじそ巻/梅じそ巻	*umejiso-maki*	Japanese *ume* plum and perilla-leaf roll
ねぎとろ巻	*negitoro-maki*	scallions-and-tuna roll
中とろ巻	*chūtoro-maki*	marbled-tuna roll
大とろ巻	*ōtoro-maki*	fatty-tuna roll
かんぴょう巻	*kanpyō-maki*	pickled-gourd rolls

太巻	*futo-maki*	a fat roll filled with rice, sweetened cooked egg, pickled gourd, and bits of vegetables
のり巻/海苔巻	*nori-maki*	same as *kanpyō-maki*; in Osaka, same as *futo-maki*
なっとう巻/ 納豆巻	*nattō-maki*	sticky, strong-tasting fermented-soybean rolls
あなきゅう巻	*ana-kyū-maki*	conger eel-and-cucumber rolls
–手巻	*-temaki*	hand-rolled cones made from dried seaweed
まぐろ手巻	*maguro-temaki*	tuna *temaki*
三色寿司	*sanshoku-zushi*	''three varieties'' of sushi or *maki-zushi*

Rice and Other Dishes

おまかせ（鮨）	*omakase(-zushi)*	selections of the chef
鉄火丼	*tekka-don*	pieces of raw tuna over rice
–丼	*-don*	over a bowl of rice
–重	*-jū*	over rice in a *bentō* box
刺身盛り合わせ	*sashimi moriawase*	regular assortment of raw fish and vegetables
さしみ/刺身 上盛り合わせ	*sashimi jō-moriawase*	deluxe assortment of raw fish
酢の物	*sunomono*	vinegared dishes
たたき/叩き	*-tataki*	pounded, almost raw fish
しおから/塩辛	*shiokara*	salted fish intestines
かわえび/川海老	*kawa-ebi*	tiny salted freshwater shrimp
（お/御）しんこ/新香	*(o)shinko*	Japanese pickles
みそ汁/味噌汁	*miso shiru*	*miso* (soybean-paste) soup

Nigiri-zushi by the Piece

Note: Japanese names of fish and seafood are shown here in *hiragana*, and sometimes *kanji*. If the actual restaurant menu uses the boxier-looking *katakana* alphabet, you may refer to the inside back cover, but it is also perfectly natural in a sushi restaurant to point to what you want in the glass case or ask for an item by name.

あじ/鯵	*aji*	horse mackerel
あか貝/赤貝	*akagai*	ark shell
あまえび/甘海老	*ama-ebi*	raw shrimp
あなご/穴子	*anago*	conger eel
あおやぎ/青柳	*aoyagi*	round clam
あわび/鮑	*awabi*	abalone
ぶり/鰤	*buri*	adult yellowtail
中とろ	*chūtoro*	marbled tuna belly
えび/海老	*ebi*	boiled shrimp
はまち/飯	*hamachi*	young yellowtail
はまぐり/蛤	*hamaguri*	clam
ひかりもの/光物	*hikari-mono*	various kinds of "shiny" fish, such as mackerel
ひも	*himo*	"fringe" around an ark shell
ひらめ/平目	*hirame*	flounder
ほっき貝	*hokkigai*	surf clam
ほたて貝/帆立貝	*hotategai*	scallop
いか	*ika*	squid
いくら/イクラ	*ikura*	salmon roe
いなだ	*inada*	very young yellowtail
貝ばしら/貝柱	*kaibashira*	shellfish valve muscles
かいわれ	*kaiware*	*daikon*-radish sprouts
かに	*kani*	crab
かんぱち/間八	*kanpachi*	very young yellowtail
かつお/鰹	*katsuo*	bonito
かずの子/数の子	*kazunoko*	herring roe
こはだ/小鰭	*kohada*	gizzard shad
くるまえび/車海老	*kuruma-ebi*	prawn
まぐろ/鮪	*maguro*	tuna
めじ	*meji (maguro)*	young tuna
みる貝	*mirugai*	surf clam
煮いか	*ni-ika*	squid simmered in a soy-flavored stock
のり玉	*nori-tama*	sweetened egg wrapped in dried seaweed

大とろ	*ōtoro*	fatty portion of tuna belly
さば/鯖	*saba*	mackerel
さより/細魚	*sayori*	(springtime) halfbeak
しゃこ	*shako*	mantis shrimp
しま鯵	*shima-aji*	another variety of *aji*
しめ鯖	*shime-saba*	mackerel (marinated)
白身	*shiromi*	seasonal "white meat" fish
すずき/鱸	*suzuki*	sea bass
たい/鯛	*tai*	sea bream
たいら貝/平貝	*tairagai*	razor-shell clam
たこ/蛸	*tako*	octopus
たまご/玉子	*tamago*	sweet egg custard wrapped in dried seaweed
とり貝/鳥貝	*torigai*	cockle
とろ	*toro*	choice tuna belly
つぶ貝	*tsubugai*	Japanese "*tsubugai*" shellfish
うに	*uni*	sea urchin roe

Other Types of Sushi (available in some places)

茶巾鮨	*chakin-zushi*	vinegared rice wrapped in a thin egg crepe
いなり鮨/稲荷鮨	*inari-zushi*	vinegared rice and vegetables wrapped in a bag of fried tofu
押し鮨	*oshi-zushi*	Osaka-style sushi: squares of pressed rice topped with vinegared/cooked fish
バッテラ(鮨)	*battera(-zushi)*	*oshi-zushi* topped with mackerel

Phrases for Ordering

I'll have some of this, please.
    Kore o kudasai.　これをください。

Two pieces of *uni* sushi, please.
    Uni o nigitte kudasai.　うにをにぎってください。

Please bring a *sashimi* platter of the best fish of the day.
Sashimi o tekitō ni mitsukurotte kudasai.
刺身を適当にみつくろってください。

One order of XX as *sashimi* (without rice), please.
XX o sashimi ni shite kudasai.
XX を刺身にしてください。

Tea, please. *Agari o kudasai.* あがりをください。

That's all for now, thank you.
Mō kekkō desu. もう結構です。

Check, please. *Oaiso o onegai shimasu.* おあいそをお願いします。

Unagi (Eel)
うなぎ・ウナギ・鰻

Grilled *unagi* is an expensive delicacy in Japan, prized not only for its flavor but also for its legendary stamina-giving properties. It's traditionally eaten during the hottest part of the summer (on the "Day of the Ox" on the lunar calendar) to provide strength and vitality for the rest of the year.

Well-prepared unagi combines a rich flavor, a bit like pâté, with an appetizing texture, crisp on the outside but succulent and tender on the inside. The cooking process is what makes the eel crisp and tender: The eels are first grilled over hot charcoal, then steamed to remove excess fat, then seasoned with a sweetish sauce and grilled a second time. In the Kansai area (around Osaka) the steaming step is omitted and the eel is grilled longer, burning off the excess fat and producing an even crisper skin.

The ingredients in the sweet basting sauce are important to the final taste of the unagi, and different restaurants maintain their own secret recipes. The quality of the charcoal used is also important: The best charcoal is made from hard oak from the south of Japan, and the aromatic smoke adds a special flavor to the eel as it's grilling.

As for the eels themselves, the best are caught wild rather than bred in eel farms, with the ideal size between 30 and 50 centimeters (12–20 inches). Fancy unagi restaurants keep tanks full of live eels, and they don't begin preparing your eel until after you've ordered. This process requires a bit of time and patience, but you're guaranteed completely fresh eel, and the results are well worth the wait.

Unagi restaurants can be recognized by an elongated (う) character (the first character in "unagi"), fashioned to resemble an eel and displayed prominently on the shop sign or curtain.

Unagi Dishes

Grilled unagi on skewers without rice is called *kabayaki*, and it's often served as an hors d'oeuvre with drinks. This same grilled unagi is also served over a bed of rice as a main course, and this comes in two varieties, called *unajū* and *unagi donburi*. Each variety comes in several different sizes.

Eel grilled without sauce is called *shirayaki*. This plain form of eel is most popular with diehard unagi purists. When you order a full-course eel meal you'll be served *kimosui*, a clear soup made from eel livers. The livers themselves are very nutritious, although not everyone enjoys the taste.

Some unagi restaurants also serve *dojō* (called loach in English), a small fish related to the eel and caught in local waters in the summer. Some restaurants specialize in dojō, while others concentrate their efforts on unagi. The best known dojō dish is *yanagawa-nabe*, a mild casserole made with boiled dojō, burdock root, and eggs.

At the table you may lightly sprinkle your unagi (or dojō) with *sanshō*, an aromatic Japanese pepper whose powdered form is most often found on unagi-restaurant tables.

UNAGI MENU

Eel Dishes

うなぎ定食/鰻定食	*unagi teishoku*	eel set meal, with skewered grilled eel, rice, pickles, and *miso* or eel-liver soup
うなずくし	*una-zukushi*	full-course eel meal (usually larger than *unagi teishoku*)
うな丼/鰻丼	*unadon*	grilled eel over rice
うな重/鰻重	*unajū*	grilled eel "piled" over rice (larger than *unadon*)
上うな重	*jō unajū*	deluxe *unajū*
梅, 竹, 松	*ume, take, matsu*	types of special sets; (see **"Reading Numbers and Basic Menu Vocabulary,"** page 45)
きもやき/肝焼	*kimoyaki*	grilled eel livers served with grated radish

かばやき/蒲焼	*kabayaki*	grilled eel on skewers (without rice)
いかだ(焼)	*ikada(yaki)*	"raft-style," with eels lined up and skewered side by side
しらやき/白焼	*shirayaki*	"white" eel, grilled plain without sauce
うなたま重	*unatama-jū*	eel and cooked egg over rice
きもすい/肝吸い	*kimosui*	clear soup made from eel livers
う巻	*umaki*	grilled eel wrapped in cooked egg
うざく	*uzaku*	grilled eel and cucumber in a soy-vinegar sauce
やわた巻/八幡巻	*yawata-maki*	grilled eel rolled around burdock strips
鰻鮨/うなぎ寿司	*unagi-zushi*	small pieces of broiled eel over rice fingers

Other Dishes Commonly Served

どじょう/どぜう	*dojō*	loach (a small eel-like fish)
やながわ鍋/柳川鍋	*yanagawa-nabe*	a casserole made with loach (or eel), burdock root, and egg
板わさ	*itawasa*	sliced *kamaboko* fish cakes served with piquant green horseradish
さしみ/刺身(盛り合わせ)	*sashimi (moriawase)*	raw fish platter
(お)造り	*(o)tsukuri*	same as *sashimi*
山かけ/山掛け	*yamakake*	grated yam over raw tuna
(若)鳥のから揚げ	*(waka)tori no kara-age*	deep-fried chicken pieces
茶づけ/茶漬	*chazuke*	green tea poured over a bowl of rice
きじ重	*kiji-jū*	grilled chicken slices over rice
おわん/お椀	*owan*	soup served in a lacquered bowl

Fugu (Blowfish)
ふぐ・フグ・河豚

If the Japanese art of food preparation sometimes tends to be theatrical, then certainly *fugu* is one of the most dramatic of foods. The fugu (known in English as the puffer, blowfish, or globefish) is a peculiar-looking fish that can puff itself up into a large, round ball when threatened by predators. Its main defense, though, is the rather toxic poison contained in its internal organs, which can be lethal to larger fish and even man. In spite of this, the non-poisonous parts of the fugu are considered an exceptional delicacy, and are relished by connoisseurs. Also, the artistic presentation of fugu dishes is quite elaborate and beautiful, even by Japanese standards.

Fugu is a seasonal dish, and it's best during the cold winter months. (This is also when the fish is at its least toxic.) It is only served in specially licensed establishments, and the poisonous parts of the fugu, including the liver and ovaries, must be carefully removed by a trained chef. Because of these precautions, accidental fugu poisoning isn't really much of a hazard anymore (although it was more of a risk in olden times). Nevertheless, fugu still retains a certain mystique, and perhaps the idea of flirting with danger, however remote, may contribute to some of the fascination with this cuisine.

Fugu restaurants are on the expensive side, and dining on fugu is regarded more as a special event than an ordinary meal. Service in fugu restaurants is usually very attentive, and the preparation of the food, needless to say, is extremely careful. Fugu may only be served between October and March, and it is at its best from December until February. Fugu is quite popular when in season, and it's always a good idea to make reservations in advance. Fugu restaurants are easy to recognize by the picture of a blowfish on the sign, and the Japanese characters (ふぐ/河豚).

Fugu Dishes

Fugu restaurants generally serve a full-course fugu meal, with the different courses representing the different textures and tastes of which fugu is capable. The first course is *fugu sashi* (*fugu sashimi*), in which the raw fugu is cut into thin, almost transparent slices. These are beautifully arranged (often in the shape of a flower) and presented on a large circular plate. A slightly sour sauce is provided for you to dip the slices into, and you also get a dish of chopped chives and grated radish with red pepper, which you may add to the dipping sauce.

In addition to *fugu sashi*, another appetizer usually served is *hirezake*, which consists of strongly flavored toasted fugu fins soaked in hot saké. The main course is *fugu chiri* (also called *chiri-nabe*), a one-pot dish similar to *shabu-shabu* (page 96) in which pieces of fugu, various vegetables, and thin noodles are boiled together. This may be cooked right at your table; the different ingredients are simply added to the hot water and stirred around until done. A small dish of sauce is provided for dipping. The fugu meal generally concludes with a soupy rice dish called *fugu zōsui*. This is made by adding rice and egg to the liquid remaining in the pot from the main course.

The menu in a fugu restaurant may also offer other winter dishes, such as *nabe* casseroles (page 92), or it may feature loach, crab, or other seafood specialties. (Refer also to the "**Izakaya/Robatayaki Menu**" on page 108 for various side dishes that may be served.)

FUGU MENU

ふぐ定食/河豚定食	*fugu teishoku*	full-course blowfish meal, with some or all of the dishes below
ふぐ刺/河豚刺	*fugu sashi*	raw blowfish, thinly sliced and artfully arranged on a tray
ふぐちり/河豚ちり	*fugu chiri*	blowfish and vegetable stew
てっちり	*tetchiri*	same as *fugu chiri*
ふぐ雑炊/河豚雑炊	*fugu zōsui*	rice porridge made with broth from *fugu chiri*
ひれ酒	*hirezake*	toasted blowfish fins in hot saké
しらこ焼	*shirako yaki*	blowfish giblets (served occasionally)

Tempura

てんぷら・テンプラ・天ぷら・天婦羅

Tempura is, in many ways, the archetypal Japanese food. All the essential elements of Japanese cuisine are reflected in the preparation of tempura: the freshness of ingredients, the art of presentation, and the perfection of technique by a skilled chef. The result is one of the triumphs of Japanese cooking—a fried food that is light and fresh-tasting rather than heavy and greasy. It's a cooking style in which the essence of the food itself completely defines the taste.

It usually comes as a great surprise to foreigners to learn that tempura was not originally Japanese at all; it actually owes its origins to the cooking style of the visiting Portuguese missionaries of the sixteenth century. Modern-day tempura is made by deep-frying vegetables, fish, and shellfish, and, like many imported ideas, it has been gradually adapted to Japanese needs and tastes. By the late nineteenth century, tempura was a popular fast food in Tokyo, available from sidewalk stalls and roaming pushcarts. A few more refinements took place since then, bringing us up to present-day tempura, no longer a foreign food but now a completely Japanese cuisine.

Preparation

Seafood and vegetables are the raw materials of tempura, and only the freshest ones are used. It's not unusual to see live shrimps jumping around on the preparation counter, or buckets of slithering eels being carted through the kitchen. The second important factor in tempura (after the freshness of the ingredients) is the quality of the batter, which is made from eggs, flour, and ice water. The batter shouldn't be mixed too thoroughly, but should be lumpy and full of air bubbles. To achieve this, the batter is made up in small batches immediately before it's used, and each batch of batter is discarded when it starts to settle.

The vegetables and seafood are cut, washed, dried, and dipped in the batter to give them a thin, almost transparent coating. After this, they're dropped one at a time into the oil (a combination of vegetable and sesame oil), which must constantly be kept at just the right temperature. Finally, the tempura must be cooked for precisely the right amount of time, and pulled out of the oil the exact moment it's done. If all goes well, the final product is perfect tempura—crisp, golden brown, hot, and delicious.

A few tempura restaurants offer variations on the basic tempura recipe, adding extra ingredients to the batter to change the texture or the taste. One variation is to add chopped noodles to the batter to create a rough and extra crisp coating.

As you can see, making tempura is a delicate process, and lots of things can go wrong. It's possible to find many different levels of quality in restaurant tempura, ranging from bad (too greasy) to absolutely perfect (heavenly). As a general rule, tempura is better at tempura specialty restaurants than at all-purpose Japanese restaurants.

Ordering and Eating

Tempura can be ordered individually by the piece, but most people order the more economical set meal (*teishoku*). The *teishoku* consists of several different varieties of tempura, plus rice, pickles, and soup. Various sizes of *teishoku* are available, and they differ in the number of pieces of tempura. The most popular seafood items include prawns, squid, shrimp, scallops, *kisu* (a type of smelt), and other kinds of fish. Many varieties of vegetable are also served, including eggplant, lotus root, green pepper, sweet potato, squash, *shiitake* mushroom, onion, *shiso* (beefsteak) leaf, and carrot. Usually some seasonal fishes are offered as well, depending on the time of year.

The first rule of dining on tempura is to eat it while it's hot. If you're sitting at the counter, the chef will transfer each piece of tempura directly from the vat of hot oil to the counter in front of you, placing it on a sheet of white rice paper to drain off the excess oil. Even if you're sitting at a table, every effort will be made to get your tempura to you as hot as possible. You can show your appreciation by eating it as soon as you can (although you might have to wait a minute or two to avoid burning your mouth).

When you use the dipping sauce, be sure to dip the tempura very quickly, and avoid lengthy soaking. The sauce may come with a small mound of grated radish, which you may mix in. Another way to eat tempura (one which some people consider more stylish) is to forgo the dipping sauce entirely. Use just a bit of salt or lemon for seasoning, and savor the pure, heavenly flavor of the tempura on its own.

TEMPURA MENU

Set Meals

てんぷら定食/ 天婦羅定食	*tenpura teishoku*	assorted pieces of tempura with rice, soup, and pickles
てんぷらコース/ 天婦羅コース	*tenpura kōsu*	a larger assortment of tempura pieces, usually with rice, soup, pickles, and dessert
てんぷら盛り合わせ/ 天婦羅盛り合わせ	*tenpura moriawase*	chef's selection of tempura pieces
(季節)野菜盛り合わせ	*(kisetsu) yasai moriawase*	assortment of (seasonal) vegetable tempura
かきあげ定食	*kakiage teishoku*	diced shrimp fried tempura-style, with rice, soup, and pickles
天丼	*tendon*	tempura-fried prawns over rice

A la Carte

Note: Seafood and vegetables served vary according to the season.

SEAFOOD:

あなご/穴子	*anago*	conger eel
えび/海老	*ebi*	shrimp
くるま海老/車海老	*kuruma-ebi*	prawn
しば海老/芝海老	*shiba-ebi*	prawn
きす	*kisu*	sillago (fish)
めごち	*megochi*	flathead (fish)

いか	*ika*	squid
帆立貝	*hotategai*	scallops
(海老)かき揚げ	*(ebi) kakiage*	diced shrimp and leek fried tempura-style
いかかき揚げ	*ika kakiage*	diced squid fried tempura-style
貝柱かき揚げ	*kaibashira kakiage*	scallop valve muscles
しらうお	*shirauo*	whitebait (fish)
しゃこ	*shako*	mantis shrimp
かに	*kani*	crab
かき/牡蠣	*kaki*	oyster (winter)
あゆ/鮎	*ayu*	sweetfish
はまぐり/蛤	*hamaguri*	clam
はぜ	*haze*	goby
やまめ	*yamame*	brown river trout
わかさぎ	*wakasagi*	freshwater smelt
-いそべ巻/ -磯辺巻	*-isobemaki*	wrapped in dried seaweed and fried
-のり巻/ -海苔巻	*-norimaki*	same as *-isobemaki*

VEGETABLES:

(季節)野菜	*(kisetsu) yasai*	(seasonal) vegetables
しいたけ/椎茸	*shiitake*	Japanese mushroom
ピーマン	*pīman*	green pepper
なす/茄子	*nasu*	eggplant
-海老詰め	*-ebizume*	stuffed with shrimp
なっとう/納豆	*nattō*	sticky, fermented soybean paste
しそ	*shiso*	perilla leaves
かぼちゃ/南瓜	*kabocha*	squash
ししとう	*shishitō*	small Japanese green pepper
さつまいも	*satsuma imo*	sweet potato
たまねぎ/玉葱	*tamanegi*	onion
にんじん/人参	*ninjin*	carrot

ごぼう	*gobō*	burdock root
アスパラ	*asupara*	asparagus
のり/海苔	*nori*	dried black seaweed
たけのこ/竹の子	*takenoko*	bamboo shoots (spring)
たらの芽	*tara no me*	buds of angelica tree (spring)
ふきのとう	*fuki no tō*	coltsfoot buds (spring)
春菊	*shungiku (no ha)*	chrysanthemum leaves (autumn)

Soba and Udon
(Buckwheat and Thick White Noodles)
そば・ソバ・蕎麦・うどん・ウドン

Soba noodles are thin, flavorful buckwheat noodles served in a light broth, and they're extremely popular for lunches, dinners, and quick snacks. Very different in character from Western-style spaghetti, soba has a richer aroma and taste and a firmer, less porous texture, so it's not as dependent on sauces to give it flavor.

There are two different styles of serving soba. The first is *kake-soba*, where the noodles are served in a bowl of hot broth with ingredients like fried tofu, vegetables, and meat. The second style is called *mori-soba*, and here the noodles are piled on bamboo screens. These plain noodles are dipped in a cold broth with scallions and green Japanese horseradish (*wasabi*). Soba noodles themselves come in different sizes and colors, including *cha-soba*, a green noodle which gets its color from the powdered green tea which is added to the buckwheat flour.

Most soba restaurants also serve another noodle called *udon*. Udon is a thick and pasty wheat noodle which is somewhat blander than soba. It's served hot (as *kake-udon*) with the same choice of topping ingredients as soba. In the Kansai region (around Osaka and Kyoto), udon is much more popular than soba, but in Tokyo soba is the favorite.

Soba Restaurants

Soba restaurants (*soba-ya*) can be recognized by the word (そば処) somewhere on the store sign, or by the piles of plastic noodles in the display window. *Soba-ya* range from cheap stand-up counters near train stations, to old, refined, and sometimes pricey restaurants that draw connoisseurs from near and far. *Soba-ya* tend to be inexpensive, though, and most family-run establishments pride themselves on developing their own unique preparation methods and combinations of ingredients.

Some of the better restaurants serve only hand-kneaded *te-uchi* (手打ち) soba, which is prized for its texture (slightly rougher and more uneven than machine-made soba). Often these shops have display windows where you can watch the soba chef actually making the noodles; it's a fascinating performance, and a guarantee of freshness.

Soba plays an important part in the New Year's holiday rituals in Japan; it's eaten on New Year's Eve for good luck (the long noodles symbolize a long life), and soba restaurants can get quite crowded then. Another soba tradition is to give a gift of soba noodles to one's new neighbors when moving into a new home (since the Japanese word "*soba*" also means "neighborhood").

Ordering and Eating

The traditional method for eating soba involves making a hearty slurping noise, accomplished by sucking in air to cool the noodles while you swallow them. This technique allows you to eat the hot noodles as quickly as possible, before they have a chance to get the least bit soggy. Correct slurping takes a bit of practice, however, so don't worry if you don't make enough noise the first time you try.

When you order, specify whether you want soba or udon (e.g. "*Kitsune soba o kudasai*"), since many items on the menu apply to both types of noodle. *Kake-soba* and *kake-udon* (in broth) may come with a dish of scallions, which you can add directly to your bowl. You can also sprinkle in *shichimi* (a powdered mixture of seven spices, including cayenne pepper), but it's rather spicy, so be careful.

When you order *mori-soba* (piled soba) it comes with a separate bowl for the dipping broth. Pour in some broth, then mix in *wasabi* (green horseradish) and chopped scallions. Dip the soba strands quickly rather than letting them soak, and don't forget to slurp; it not only allows you to taste the broth, but helps to cool off the hot noodles to a more enjoyable temperature as well. Near the end of the meal the waiter will sometimes bring a pitcher of the hot water in which the noodles were cooked. After you've finished your noodles you can use the hot water to dilute the dipping broth if you want to drink it.

Most *soba-ya* also serve rice-based dishes without noodles, some of which are listed at the end of the menu section. (The variety of fried noodles known as *yakisoba* is actually made from Chinese *rāmen* noodles rather than soba; it can often be found in Chinese restaurants, *okonomiyaki* restaurants, and at *yakisoba* stands.)

SOBA MENU

Hot Noodles in Broth (Soba and Udon)

Note: Choose soba or udon when ordering, unless one or the other is specifically listed on the menu. The main topping ingredients are listed below; other ingredients may include various fish cakes, chopped spinach, scallions, trefoil leaf, etc.

かけ/掛け	*kake*	plain noodles (soba or udon) in hot broth (fish and soy-sauce-flavored)
たぬき	*tanuki*	fried tempura batter topping (lit. ''badger'')
きつね	*kitsune*	fried tofu topping (lit. ''fox'')
月見	*tsukimi*	raw egg and dried seaweed topping (lit. ''moon-viewing,'' since the egg resembles the moon in appearance)
玉子とじ	*tamago toji*	cooked egg-and-fish-cake topping
おかめ	*okame*	fish cakes, mushrooms, bamboo shoots, and wheat cakes arranged over noodles
おかめとじ	*okame toji*	*okame* ingredients with egg
あんかけ	*ankake*	*okame* ingredients in a sauce that is thicker and sweeter than usual (winter specialty)
かき玉	*kakitama*	egg in a cornstarch-thickened broth
わかめ	*wakame*	seaweed topping

なめこ	nameko	tiny, slithery-textured mushrooms
山菜	sansai	assorted "mountain vegetables," including bracken, flowering fern, dropwort, etc.
山かけ/山掛け	yamakake	grated yam sauce topping
とろろ	tororo	same as yamakake (but sometimes made of grated taro potato)
けんちん	kenchin	taro (potato), pork, konnyaku, and burdock root
にしん	nishin	herring (Osaka-region specialty)
力	chikara	mochi (pounded rice cakes)
スタミナ	sutamina	eggs, mochi, and other stamina-producing ingredients
肉南蛮	niku nanban	meat (usually pork) and leek topping
カレー南蛮	karē nanban	leeks and curry-flavored sauce
かも南蛮/鴨南蛮	kamo nanban	chicken (lit. "duck") and leek topping
親子南蛮	oyako nanban	chicken and egg (lit. "parent and child") and leek topping
天南蛮	ten nanban	tempura-fried shrimp and leek topping
てんぷら/ 天婦羅(そば)	tenpura soba	tempura-fried shrimp topping
てんとじ/天とじ	ten toji	tempura-fried shrimp and egg topping
なべやきうどん/ 鍋焼うどん	nabeyaki udon	casserole-style dish with mushrooms, assorted vegetables, egg, and sometimes tempura-style shrimp (winter specialty)
すきやきうどん/ すき焼うどん	sukiyaki udon	same as nabeyaki udon, but with beef instead of shrimp (winter specialty)

ぞうに/雑煮	zōni	mochi (pounded rice cakes) and assorted vegetables
おろし	oroshi	grated daikon
なっとう/納豆	nattō	fermented, sticky soybean-paste topping
五目	gomoku	(lit. "five ingredients") Chinese-style with boiled egg, fish cakes, vegetables, pork and ham topping
きしめん	kishimen	thin, wide white wheat noodles, similar to udon, but flatter
–とじ	-toji	with egg
–なんばん/–南蛮	-nanban	with leek
みそ–/味噌–	miso-	with miso sauce
天–	ten-	with tempura-style fried shrimp

(**Note**: Your menu may also include combinations of the above ingredients, e.g., chikara tanuki or kitsune toji.)

Cold Noodles (Soba Only)

もり/盛り	mori	soba noodles piled on a bamboo rack in a lacquer box
大もり/大盛り	ōmori	large portion of mori soba (when this term appears with another dish, it just means "large portion")
ざる	zaru	mori soba topped with dried seaweed strips
大ざる	ōzaru	large portion of zaru soba
天ざる	ten zaru	hot tempura-style shrimp served with cold zaru soba
せいろ	seiro	can be the same as zaru or mori, depending on the shop
冷したぬき	hiyashi tanuki	cold soba with bits of tempura batter (summer specialty)

冷しきつね	*hiyashi kitsune*	cold soba with fried tofu (summer)
冷し中華	*hiyashi chūka*	cold Chinese-style noodles in sesame-vinegar sauce with strips of cucumber, ham, and fish cakes (summer)
ひやむぎ/冷麦	*hiyamugi*	thin white wheat noodles served in a bowl of cold water with strips of cucumber or other garnish (summer)
冷し-	*hiyashi-*	cold noodle versions of various toppings listed in hot-noodle section above
そーめん	*sōmen*	similar to *hiyamugi*, but thinner (summer)

(**Note:** Other toppings from the hot-noodle section may also be listed in the cold-noodle section on your menu.)

Rice Dishes Served at Soba Restaurants

ライス	*raisu*	plain white rice
カレーライス	*karē raisu*	rice topped with curry-flavored sauce, bits of meat, vegetables, pickles, etc.
カレー丼	*karē don(buri)*	similar to *karē raisu*, but served in a round *donburi* bowl
親子丼	*oyako don*	chicken and egg topping over rice (lit. "parent and child")
かつ丼	*katsu don*	pork cutlet and egg over rice in a round bowl
かつ重	*katsu jū*	pork cutlet and egg over rice in a rectangular box
天丼	*ten don*	tempura-style shrimp over rice
玉子丼	*tamago don*	cooked egg topping over rice
開化丼	*kaika don*	pork slices and egg over rice
うな玉丼	*unatama don*	grilled eel and egg over rice

Other Menu Items

（お）しんこ	(o)shinko	pickled white cabbage, radish, eggplant, and/or cucumber
みそ汁/味噌汁	miso shiru	soup flavored with miso (soy paste)
ビール	bīru	beer
定食	teishoku	set meal with rice and miso soup
並	nami	regular size
大盛り	ōmori	large size

Tonkatsu (Pork Cutlets)
とんかつ ・ トンカツ ・ 豚カツ

Tonkatsu (deep-fried pork cutlet) is, like tempura, another Japanese dish that finds its origins in Western cooking. Like tempura, it underwent a long history of refinement and adaptation to Japanese tastes, until eventually the art of tonkatsu preparation was transformed into a uniquely Japanese cooking style.

Tonkatsu is made by cutting pork filets into thick slices, breading them heavily, then deep-frying them slowly until the breading layer is light brown and crunchy. The thick outer crust on a well-prepared tonkatsu is surprisingly un-greasy, and its crisp texture provides a satisfying contrast with the naturally juicy meat inside.

Exactly why this particular style of cooking pork caught on so firmly in Japan is hard to explain, but catch on it did, practically to the exclusion of all other pork dishes. In fact, tonkatsu is so popular that *tonkatsu-ya* (tonkatsu restaurants) are among the most common restaurants in Japan.

Tonkatsu-ya are relatively inexpensive, and this is certainly one reason for their popularity. They can be recognized either by the word tonkatsu (とんかつ), or by some sort of pig motif on the sign. The basic cooking method for tonkatsu is always the same, so different shops distinguish themselves by the quality of the meat, the ingredients in the breading, and the color and crispness of the finished product.

Tonkatsu Dishes

The usual meal in a tonkatsu restaurant is some sort of *teishoku*, a set meal consisting of tonkatsu, rice, soup, pickles, and a large heap of shredded raw cabbage. Two grades of meat are used for tonkatsu: the less expensive *rōsu katsu* (derived from the word "roast"), on which some of the fat is left untrimmed before cooking, and the choicer *hire katsu* (from the word "fillet"), a leaner cut of pork from which the fat is fully trimmed before cooking.

Many other popular deep-fried dishes are served in *tonkatsu-ya*. Among these are *korokke*, croquettes made from mashed potatoes, ground meat, onions, corn, or crabmeat in cream sauce. *Menchi-katsu*, made with ground beef, is essentially a deep-fried hamburger. Chicken cutlets, fried shrimp, and fried fish are sometimes served, as are various *kushiage* specialties: pork, vegetables, and other foods which are skewered before being deep-fried.

Tonjiru, a tasty *miso* soup made with pieces of pork and chopped vegetables, is often available as an alternative to the ever-present *miso-shiru* (soybean-paste soup). Condiments on your table will include a strong yellowish mustard and two special tonkatsu sauces, which may be poured directly over your tonkatsu. One is a thick, sweetish sauce, while the other is much thinner and tastes like Worcestershire sauce. The better tonkatsu shops make their own sauces from closely guarded secret recipes, and some of the larger shops bottle their sauces for home use.

Tonkatsu restaurants, in addition to the foods on the sample menu in this section, may also serve items from the **"Kushiage Menu"** (see page 82).

TONKATSU MENU

Meat Dishes

ロースかつ	*rōsu katsu*	deep-fried pork cutlet with fatty portion included
ロースかつ定食	*rōsu katsu teishoku*	*rōsu katsu* set meal with rice, pickles, and soup
上ロースかつ	*jō rōsu katsu*	deluxe portion of *rōsu katsu*
ひれかつ /ヒレカツ	*hire katsu*	lean pork cutlet
一口ひれかつ /一口ヒレカツ	*hito-kuchi hire katsu*	bite-size chunks of lean pork
かつ重	*katsu jū*	pork cutlet over rice
串かつ	*kushi katsu*	fatty chunks of pork and leek on skewers

チキンかつ	chikin katsu	tender chicken cutlet (deep-fried)
鳥から揚げ/鳥唐揚げ	tori kara-age	chicken pieces deep-fried without batter
わかどり/若鳥	waka-dori	(young) chicken
メンチかつ	menchi katsu	deep-fried ground-meat patty
コロッケ	korokke	potato and/or crab croquette
かにコロッケ	kani korokke	crab croquette
えびフライ/海老フライ	ebi furai	deep-fried shrimp
ミックスフライ	mikkusu furai	deep-fried assortment with shrimp, croquette, and/or pork
かきフライ	kaki furai	deep-fried oysters (winter)
チーズかつ	chīzu katsu	pork cutlet with cheese
かつサンド	katsu sando	pork cutlet sandwich

Side Dishes

生野菜	nama yasai	shredded cabbage, tomato, and lettuce salad
みそ汁/味噌汁	miso shiru	miso (soy paste) soup
赤だし	akadashi	red-miso soup
とん汁/豚汁	ton-jiru	miso soup with pork and chopped vegetables
なめこ汁	nameko-jiru	broth flavored with tiny mushrooms
(お/御)しんこ/新香	(o)shinko	a dish of pickled white cabbage, cucumber, radish, and/or eggplant
ライス	raisu	plain white rice (steamed)

Useful Vocabulary

ソース	sōsu	sauce
甘ロー	amakuchi-	thick, sweet sauce
辛ロー	karakuchi-	thin Worcestershire-like sauce
しょうゆ	shōyu	soy sauce
からし/辛子	karashi	mustard

Kushiage (Skewered Foods)
くしあげ・串揚

Kushiage is cooked the same way as deep-fried pork *tonkatsu*, but the ingredients used are completely different. In kushiage cooking, prawns, scallops, large *shiitake* mushrooms, and many other kinds of seafoods, meats, and vegetables are skewered on long bamboo sticks. These skewered foods are then breaded and deep-fried like *tonkatsu*. And the results are just as good: The fresh texture and taste of the ingredients are perfectly preserved under the layer of breading, which adds a delicious flavor and crunchiness of its own.

Since kushiage is so similar to *tonkatsu* in preparation, it's often served in *tonkatsu* restaurants. There are also specialty kushiage restaurants, which can be recognized by the word *kushiage* (串揚) on the sign. The Japanese character for *kushi* (串), which means skewer, is one of the easiest to remember, since it looks like two pieces of food arranged on a skewer. Kushiage is a popular side dish when drinking, so kushiage restaurants often have a pub-style atmosphere in keeping with this custom.

Almost any kind of food can be cooked kushiage-style, and many restaurants offer unusual selections on their menus. The most common items include prawns, squid, scallops, and other seafood, as well as green peppers, large *shiitake* mushrooms, and other vegetables. Some of the fun of eating kushiage is the surprise of finding out just what's hiding underneath the layer of breading.

There are two ways to order kushiage, either by the individual skewer or in combinations of anywhere from five to twenty or more skewers, depending on your appetite and your budget. (The larger combination plates are shared by everyone at the table, and are eaten while drinking beer or saké.) It's usually more economical to order a combination plate (usually called a *kushiage kōsu*, or "course"), and some restaurants don't even have an a la carte menu. If you do order a la carte, you will generally be served two skewers of any individual item. Kushiage restaurants provide one or more specially made sauces to dip your food in, and wedges of lemon are served as well.

Kushiage can be found in specialty kushiage restaurants, *tonkatsu* restaurants, pubs, and a few *yakitori* restaurants.

KUSHIAGE MENU

Combination Platters

串揚コース	*kushiage kōsu*	a preselected assortment of kushiage skewers
（七)本	*(nana) hon*	(seven) sticks

A la Carte Items

えび/海老	*ebi*	shrimp
帆立貝	*hotategai*	scallops
いか	*ika*	squid
げそ/下足	*geso*	squid tentacles
きす	*kisu*	sillago (similar to smelt)
つみれ	*tsumire*	fish cake
はんぺん/半ぺん	*hanpen*	soft white fish cake
しいたけ/椎茸	*shiitake*	Japanese mushrooms
うずら/鶉（玉子)	*uzura (tamago)*	quail eggs
はす	*hasu*	lotus root
れんこん/蓮根	*renkon*	lotus root
ぎんなん/銀杏	*ginnan*	ginkgo nuts
おくら/オクラ	*okura*	okra
なす/茄子	*nasu*	eggplant
とうふ/豆腐	*tōfu*	bean curd
こんにゃく	*konnyaku*	block of devil's-tongue starch
チーズ	*chīzu*	cheese
たまねぎ/玉葱	*tamanegi*	onion

いも/芋	*imo*	potato
えのき （ーベーコン巻）	*enoki* (*-bēkon maki*)	thin white mushrooms (wrapped in bacon)
ピーマン	*pīman*	green pepper
ピーマン肉詰め	*pīman niku-zume*	green pepper stuffed with ground meat
ししとう	*shishitō*	Japanese green pepper (small)
アスパラ	*asupara*	asparagus
ーベーコン巻	*-bēkon-maki*	wrapped in bacon
ーしそ巻	*-shiso-maki*	wrapped in *shiso* (perilla) leaf
牛肉	*gyū niku*	beef
豚肉	*buta niku*	pork
ささみ(ー巻)	*sasami (-maki)*	(rolled) boneless chicken breast
ウインナー	*uinnā*	cocktail wieners

Other Dishes

Note: Please also refer to the **"Izakaya/Robatayaki Menu"** on page 108 for other food items.

さしみ/刺身 （盛り合わせ）	*sashimi* (*moriawase*)	raw fish assorted platter
やきとり/焼鳥	*yakitori*	grilled chicken (see **"Yakitori Menu,"** page 85)
おにぎり	*onigiri*	rice ball wrapped in dried seaweed
焼おにぎり	*yaki-onigiri*	roasted rice ball (without seaweed)

Useful Phrases

More sauce, please.

　　Sōsu o motto kudasai.　ソースをもっとください。

Two sticks of XX, please.

　　XX o ni-hon kudasai.　XX を2本ください。

Yakitori (Grilled Chicken)
やきとり・ヤキトリ・焼とり・焼鳥

Succulent pieces of skewered chicken, dipped in barbecue sauce, grilled to perfection over hot charcoal, then washed down with a cold beer—it's easy to see the appeal of *yakitori* after a hard day's work. Not surprisingly, *yakitori-ya* (yakitori restaurants and stands) are popular early-evening gathering places, usually filled with office workers stopping for snacks before the train ride home.

Yakitori-ya themselves are far from fancy; often they'll consist of just five or six stools pushed up against a counter. Clouds of aromatic smoke waft off the grill and into the street to lure hungry passersby. Even at the nicer places, the emphasis isn't on the decor; they're more interested in providing good food and a convivial, relaxed atmosphere in which to enjoy eating.

Yakitori-ya can be recognized by small red lanterns out front, with the character for *tori*, or bird (鳥), or the syllabic spelling of "yakitori" やきとり). (On the other hand, if you see large red lanterns out front, it may indicate an ordinary pub-style restaurant; see page 107.) Another clue to finding a *yakitori-ya* is the clouds of fragrant smoke coming from the vent.

The two main factors that set one *yakitori-ya* apart from the next are the ingredients in the *tare* (the sauce used to baste the chicken) and the quality of the charcoal used for grilling. Hard, aromatic charcoal from Wakayama Prefecture produces the best results, better than cheaper charcoals and far superior to gas or electric grills.

Yakitori Dishes

Although other foods are served, chicken is the mainstay of *yakitori-ya*. Morsels of chicken are either skewered by themselves or interspersed with *negi* (similar to a leek) or other vegetables. Other chicken dishes include skewered chicken wings, tender white-meat chicken breast fillets (*sasami*), dark-meat chicken-leg chunks, chicken livers and other organs, ground-chicken meatballs (*tsukune*), and even chicken skin. There are also other items, such as large *shiitake* mushrooms, green peppers, ginkgo nuts, and small quail eggs.

All food served in *yakitori-ya* comes on skewers, and you will usually receive two skewers of any item you order. Before it's grilled, the food is dipped into either a sweetish soy-based sauce (*tare*) or salt (*shio*)—sometimes you get a choice, but often one or the other is the specialty of the chef. You can also sprinkle your chicken with *shichimi* (a mixture of red pepper and six other spices). Usually you'll find a handy receptacle on the counter where you can deposit your used skewers.

Some fancy places have a wider variety of food choices, with more exotic delicacies like asparagus, rabbit, or sparrow, but generally the smaller restaurants and stands limit themselves to basics. Most patrons drink beer with their yakitori, although soft drinks are usually available. After you've had enough chicken, *chazuke* (a soupy mixture of tea and rice) is a very filling way to top off the meal.

Yakitori is served at specialty yakitori restaurants and many other eating places, often in conjunction with *kamameshi* (see page 90) or *kushiage* (see page 82).

YAKITORI MENU

A la Carte Items (by the Skewer)

CHICKEN AND OTHER MEAT:

やきとり/焼鳥	*yakitori*	grilled, skewered chicken pieces
はさみ	*hasami*	alternating pieces of chicken and leek
ねぎま	*negima*	chicken pieces and leek
ささみ	*sasami*	chicken breast meat (without skin)
正肉	*shōniku*	boneless meat with skin
なんこつ	*nankotsu*	chicken pieces with bone

てばさき/手羽先	*tebasaki*	chicken wings
つくね	*tsukune*	chicken meatballs
もも(焼)	*momo (yaki)*	chicken legs
かわ/皮	*kawa*	chicken skin
すなぎも/砂肝	*sunagimo*	gizzards
はつ/ハツ	*hatsu*	hearts
もつ/モツ	*motsu*	giblets
レバー	*rebā*	chicken livers
とりきも焼/ 鳥肝焼	*tori kimo yaki*	chicken livers and other giblets
ぼんちり	*bonchiri*	chicken tail
ひな(鳥)	*hina (dori)*	very young chicken
骨付き	*hone tsuki*	bones included
あいがも/合鴨	*aigamo*	duck (a cross between a wild and a domestic duck)
すずめ	*suzume*	sparrow (or young chicken)
うずら/鶉(玉子)	*uzura (tamago)*	quail eggs
たん/タン	*tan*	beef tongue

VEGETABLES:

野菜焼	*yasai yaki*	grilled, skewered vegetables
ねぎ/葱	*negi*	leek
ピーマン	*pīman*	green pepper
ししとう	*shishitō*	Japanese green pepper (small)
ぎんなん/銀杏	*ginnan*	ginkgo nuts
たまねぎ/玉葱	*tamanegi*	onion
しいたけ/椎茸	*shiitake*	Japanese mushrooms

Other Dishes

Note: Please refer also to the "**Izakaya/Robatayaki Menu**" on page 108.

(焼鳥)コース	*(yakitori) kōsu*	a preselected assortment of various yakitori skewers
とりわさ/鳥わさ	*tori-wasa*	almost-raw chicken pieces, served with Japanese horseradish

とり刺/鳥刺	*tori-sashi*	raw chicken, served *sashimi-*style
から揚げ/唐揚げ	*kara-age*	deep-fried chicken
煮込み	*nikomi*	meat and vegetable stew
やながわ鍋/柳川鍋	*yanagawa nabe*	casserole made with eel/loach, burdock root, and egg
-なべ/鍋	*-nabe*	quick-cooked stew (*see* "**Nabemono Menu**," page 93)
串揚	*kushiage*	skewered, deep-fried foods (*see* "**Kushiage Menu**," page 82)
やきとり丼/焼鳥丼	*yakitori don*	grilled chicken pieces over rice
きじ焼丼	*kiji-yaki don*	grilled chicken pieces over rice
-丼	*-don*	various rice dishes (*see* last section of "**Soba Menu**," page 76)

Rice and Side Dishes

釜めし	*kamameshi*	steamed rice with seafood and vegetables (see "**Kamameshi Menu**," page 90)
茶づけ/茶漬	*chazuke*	a soupy mixture of rice and green tea with various ingredients (see below)
とり/鳥-	*tori-*	(almost raw) chicken
さけ/鮭-	*sake-*	salmon
うめ/梅-	*ume-*	Japanese plum
のり/海苔-	*nori-*	dried seaweed
たらこ-	*tarako-*	cod roe
おにぎり	*onigiri*	rice ball wrapped in dried seaweed
焼おにぎり	*yaki-onigiri*	roasted rice ball (without seaweed)
ライス	*raisu*	rice

(お/御)しんこ/ 新香	(o)shinko	Japanese-style pickles
生野菜	nama yasai	raw vegetables
キャベツ	kyabetsu	cabbage
きゅうり	kyūri	cucumber

Useful Vocabulary

two skewers   *ni-hon*   二本

four skewers   *yon-hon*   四本

Would you like that *tare*-style or *shio*-style (basted in sauce or salted)?
  Tare-aji ni shimasu ka? Shio-aji ni shimasu ka?
  タレ味にしますか，塩味にしますか？

With sauce, please.
  Tare-aji de onegai shimasu.   タレ味でおねがいします。

With salt, please.
  Shio-aji de onegai shimasu.   塩味でおねがいします。

Kamameshi (Rice Dishes)

かまめし・釜飯・釜めし

Rice is not only Japan's most important food, it is also an essential element in Japanese history, mythology, and cultural identity. It shouldn't be surprising, then, to find an entire cuisine based on rice dishes.

The word *kamameshi* refers simply to rice (*meshi*) which is cooked in a special iron pot (*kama*), but kamameshi dishes are much more elaborate than ordinary steamed rice. The rice itself is flavored with soy sauce and other seasonings, and it's mixed and topped with finely chopped mushrooms, seafood, bamboo shoots, and other vegetables. The rice turns a light brown color from the seasonings, and it absorbs the flavor of the other ingredients as everything is steam-cooked together. The finished kamameshi has some of the appearance and character of a paella dish, although it's more uniform and subdued in taste. Many Westerners find it somewhat unexciting as a main dish, and prefer it as a side dish.

Kamameshi is served in a small, old-fashioned metal pot which is housed in a distinctive square wooden frame and covered with a round lid. The various ingredients are carefully arranged on top of the rice, and often have contrasting colors and textures. Restaurants which specialize in kamameshi tend to have a rustic, or at least traditional, atmosphere. Kamameshi is often served with *yakitori*, since *yakitori* by itself is not all that filling; *yakitori* restaurants and kamameshi restaurants often serve both specialties.

Popular ingredients for kamameshi include crab, scallops, shrimp, chicken, different varieties of mushrooms and edible fungi, and finely chopped vegetables. Kamameshi can be ordered either a la carte or as the centerpiece of a combination meal, which may include a steamed egg custard, a few skewers of *yakitori*, or even tempura.

Kamameshi can be found in specialty *yakitori* and kamameshi restaurants, and also in many traditional and regional-style Japanese restaurants.

KAMAMESHI MENU

Kamameshi Dishes

釜めし/釜飯	*kamameshi*	seasoned, steamed rice with various ingredients
-釜めし定食	*-kamameshi teishoku*	set meal with kamameshi, soup, pickles, and possibly other dishes
-御膳	*-gozen*	set meal with kamameshi and other foods, such as *yakitori*

TOPPING INGREDIENTS:

かに	*kani*	crabmeat
とり/鳥	*tori*	chicken
あさり	*asari*	short-necked clams
さけ/鮭	*sake*	salmon
五目	*gomoku*	"five ingredients": bits of various vegetables, seafood, and chicken
三色	*sanshoku*	"three colors": pink-colored powdered cod meat, crumbled boiled egg, and vegetables
帆立貝	*hotategai*	scallops
貝柱	*kaibashira*	scallop valve muscles
あわび	*awabi*	abalone
えび/海老	*ebi*	shrimp
かき/牡蠣	*kaki*	oysters (winter)
牛(肉)	*gyū (niku)*	beef
山菜	*sansai*	"mountain vegetables": bracken, flowering fern, etc.
くり/栗	*kuri*	chestnuts
しいたけ/椎茸	*shiitake*	Japanese mushrooms
まつたけ/松茸	*matsutake*	choice pine mushrooms
たけのこ/竹の子	*takenoko*	bamboo shoots

Other Dishes

かに雑炊	kani zōsui	rice soup with crabmeat
とり雑炊	tori zōsui	rice soup with chicken
玉子雑炊	tamago zōsui	egg-flavored rice soup
刺身(盛り合わせ)	sashimi (moriawase)	assorted raw fish platter
やきとり/焼鳥	yakitori	chicken and other items broiled on skewers (see "**Yakitori Menu**," page 85)
串焼	kushiyaki	yakitori and other skewered foods (see "**Yakitori Menu**," page 85)

Nabemono (Quick-Cooked Stews)
なべ・ナベ・鍋(物)

Nabemono dishes are hearty wintertime favorites, prepared from fish, seafood, chicken, or meat and vegetables in a bubbling caldron right at your table. Serving trays are piled high with raw ingredients and brought to the table, then everyone cooks the stew together and eats out of the communal pot. The atmosphere at nabemono restaurants is down-to-earth, and often the decor features a rustic theme, reflecting nabemono's origins in Japan's rural farming regions.

There are lots of different kinds of nabemono, depending on the ingredients used. Stews featuring oysters, scallops, cod, salmon, turtle, and chicken are all popular. The variety known as *chanko-nabe* (containing chicken, seafood, potatoes, and other vegetables) makes up the staple diet of Japan's sumo wrestlers. *Chanko-nabe* is, as you might expect, quite filling. Another special variety of nabemono is the well-known beef sukiyaki (see page 96).

Since *nabe* dishes are cooked quickly, the ingredients retain their individual flavor and identity. The nabemono, then, presents a succession of different tastes and textures as the various vegetables and morsels of seafood are pulled out of the pot and eaten. As the meal progresses, the cooking liquid absorbs more and more flavors (especially from the fish or meat).

Eating Nabemono

Dining on nabemono is a participatory experience, since everyone at the table does the cooking (although sometimes the restaurant staff helps out). It's very easy to prepare, and the process can be entertaining as well. Tables at nabemono restaurants are each equipped with a small gas burner (or a portable charcoal *hibachi* burner at traditional places). The burner is lit and a big pot of cooking broth is set on top. Once the liquid starts bubbling you can add the food to the pot, piece by piece.

The fish, prawns, and various mushrooms and fungi should be added first, since they take the longest to cook. Very crisp vegetables, such as carrots, can also be added at this stage. Seasonings such as scallions, grated radish, and red pepper are usually added to your own private dish of *ponzu tare* (a citron-flavored soy-base dip) rather than to the communal pot.

The most delicate foods (such as tofu and chrysanthemum leaves) should be cooked just before you eat them. Watch them carefully and pull them out quickly, otherwise they'll overcook and fall apart. Some stews come with *udon* noodles, which you may cook toward the end of your meal. Rice may also be added to the *nabe* (pot) at the end, creating a kind of rice porridge from the remaining liquid.

Your waitress will come by occasionally to make sure that everything's okay. You can ask her to turn down the flame on your burner or solicit advice on whether your stew is fully cooked and ready to eat, especially if you're a first-time nabemono chef. The waitress may skim the foam off the top of the liquid with a wooden skimming spoon, although usually you're left to do this yourself.

Nabemono dishes are mostly served during the late fall and winter months. A few varieties, such as beef sukiyaki, may be found in other seasons as well. Nabemono can be ordered in specialty nabemono establishments, pub-type restaurants, some *fugu* restaurants, and many other eateries. (Refer also to the "**Sukiyaki and Shabu-shabu**" and "**Oden**" chapters.) Exotic meats such as wild boar, venison, and even horsemeat are often cooked nabemono-style. Some of these are listed in the sample menu below, and these dishes can also be found in certain regional specialty restaurants.

NABEMONO MENU

Nabemono (Quick-Cooked Stews)

すきやき/好き焼 *sukiyaki*	thinly sliced beef and vegetables (*see also* "**Sukiyaki and Shabu-shabu**" on page 96)

しゃぶしゃぶ	*shabu-shabu*	thinly sliced beef quick-cooked in a watery broth (*see* page 96)
寄せ鍋	*yose-nabe*	vegetable and seafood (and/or chicken) stew
ちり鍋	*chiri-nabe*	fish and vegetable stew
たら(ちり)鍋	*tara (chiri)-nabe*	codfish and vegetable stew
かき鍋	*kaki-nabe*	oyster and vegetable stew
どて鍋/土手鍋	*dote-nabe*	oyster and vegetable stew with *miso* (soybean paste)
水炊き	*mizutaki*	chicken and vegetable stew
やながわ鍋/柳川鍋	*yanagawa-nabe*	stew made from loach, burdock root, and egg
どじょう鍋/どぜう鍋	*dojō-nabe*	same as *yanagawa-nabe*
湯豆腐	*yudōfu*	tofu boiled in hot water
うどんすき	*udon-suki*	fat *udon* noodles and fish stew
あんこう鍋/鮟鱇鍋	*ankō-nabe*	angler-fish stew
かも鍋/鴨鍋	*kamo-nabe*	duck (or chicken [dark meat]) stew
すっぽん鍋	*suppon-nabe*	softshelled-turtle stew
いしかり鍋/石狩鍋	*ishikari-nabe*	salmon and vegetable stew with *miso* (soybean paste) and butter
さくら鍋/桜鍋	*sakura-nabe*	horsemeat stew
ぼたん鍋/牡丹鍋	*botan-nabe*	wild-boar stew
いのしし鍋/猪鍋	*inoshishi-nabe*	same as *botan-nabe*

Chanko-nabe

ちゃんこ鍋	*chanko-nabe*	hearty, filling stew made of various ingredients, eaten by sumo wrestlers
とり肉/鳥肉	*tori niku*	with chicken
さかな/魚	*sakana*	with fish
ぶた肉/豚肉	*buta niku*	with pork
えび/海老	*ebi*	with shrimp
牛肉	*gyū niku*	with beef

Useful Vocabulary and Phrases

雑炊	*zōsui*	rice gruel (sometimes added to *nabe* broth at the end of the meal)
うどん	*udon*	fat noodles (sometimes added to *nabe* broth at the end of the meal)

Please turn (up/down) the flame.
Hi o (tsuyoku/yowaku) shite kudasai.
火を（強く/弱く）してください。

Please turn off the burner.
Hi o tomete kudasai. 火を止めてください。

Do you think this is done yet?
Mō taberaremasu ka? もう食べられますか？

Yes. *Hai, (taberaremasu).* はい，（食べられます）。

Not yet. *Iie./Mada.* いいえ。/まだ。

Sukiyaki and Shabu-shabu
(Beef Hotpot Dishes)

すきやき・スキヤキ・好き焼・鋤焼・
しゃぶしゃぶ・シャブシャブ

When beef-eating was introduced to Japan in the mid-1800's, the most popular beef dish was the familiar one-pot, *nabemono*-style stew. Present-day sukiyaki is very close to the beef *nabemono* of the last century, and it continues to be a popular (though expensive) wintertime delicacy.

Specialty sukiyaki restaurants are often run by meat companies. They tend to be discreet in their exterior advertising, and fancier than average in their interior decor (reflecting the high price of the beef they serve). They can be recognized by the word "*sukiyaki*" (すき焼) or by drawings of cows.

Sukiyaki is usually prepared at your table, but unlike many other nabemono dishes, you don't have to cook it yourself. To make sukiyaki, you first take very thin slices of marbled beef and fry them lightly in fat. When they're sufficiently browned, a cooking stock flavored with soy sauce, sweetened saké, and sugar is poured into the pan. The other ingredients (leeks, grilled tofu, *shiitake* mushrooms, and transparent noodles) are added, and everything is brought to a boil. Finally, chrysanthemum leaves are added and cooked very briefly. When the sukiyaki is ready, everyone at the table can start fishing out their favorite morsels of food from the common pot. Each person also receives a small dish containing a raw egg; beat the egg in the dish and dip the cooked meat into it before eating.

Sukiyaki restaurants also serve another beef hotpot dish called *shabu-shabu*. This is a dish which you cook for yourself, using many of the same ingredients as sukiyaki. A doughnut-shaped cooking pan filled with light broth is heated at your table, and then you dip very thinly sliced beef and various vegetables into the boiling liquid. The slices of beef are so thin that they cook in a matter of seconds, so be careful not to overcook them. Two contrasting sauces are provided for dipping: One is slightly tart and citrus-flavored, while the other is a thicker sesame-based sauce. Some restaurants also serve a crab version of shabu-shabu.

In addition to specialty sukiyaki restaurants, there are also restaurants that specialize solely in shabu-shabu. Both these dishes can also be found in many *nabemono* restaurants and other establishments, particularly during the colder months of the year.

SUKIYAKI AND SHABU-SHABU MENU

Sukiyaki

(上)すきやき/ 好き焼	(*jō*) *sukiyaki*	thinly sliced beef and vegetables (special portion)
しもふり/霜降 すきやき	*shimofuri sukiyaki*	choice marbled-beef sukiyaki
ヒレすきやき	*hire sukiyaki*	beef-fillet sukiyaki
ロースすきやき	*rōsu sukiyaki*	sukiyaki of ordinary cut of beef
松坂牛(肉)	*Matsuzaka gyū* (*niku*)	choice beef from Matsuzaka; also known in the West as Kobe beef
近江牛(肉)	*Ōmi gyū* (*niku*)	choice beef from Shiga-ken (near Kyoto)
神戸牛(肉)	*Kōbe gyū* (*niku*)	choice beef from Kobe (same as Matsuzaka beef)

Shabu-shabu

しゃぶしゃぶ	*shabu-shabu*	thinly sliced beef quick-cooked in watery broth
(上)牛ロース	(*jō*) *gyū rōsu*	(deluxe portion) of beef
野菜盛り合わせ	*yasai moriawase*	extra vegetables to add to the shabu-shabu pot (bok choy, mushrooms, chrysanthemum leaves, etc.)

Otsumami (Snacks)

Note: Refer also to the *Otsumami* section of the **"Izakaya and Robatayaki Menu,"** page 111.

牛刺（身）	*gyū sashi(mi)*	thinly sliced raw beef
牛（肉）たたき	*gyū (niku) tataki*	thinly sliced, almost raw beef
あじたたき/鯵たたき	*aji tataki*	thinly sliced, almost raw horse mackerel
刺身盛り合わせ	*sashimi moriawase*	platter of assorted raw fish
茶そば/茶蕎麦	*chasoba*	green-tea-flavored *soba* noodles
雑炊	*zōsui*	rice gruel (sometimes made by adding rice to the cooking broth at the end of the meal)

Useful Phrases

Please turn (up/down) the flame.
Hi o (tsuyoku/yowaku) shite kudasai.
火を（強く/弱く）してください。

Please turn off the burner.
Hi o tomete kudasai.　火を止めてください。

Oden (Fish-Cake Stews)
おでん・オデン

When mid-autumn comes to Japan and the days start getting cooler, a cherished seasonal sight is the return of the *oden* stalls to city sidewalks. Oden is a very simple stew made by simmering assorted fish dumplings, fried tofu, eggs, and vegetables in a kelp-based stock for hours on end. It's popular and inexpensive cold-weather nourishment, and every night droves of tiny sidewalk stands descend on train stations and entertainment areas to meet the demand. Sidewalk stalls usually feature a tiny counter with four or five stools and a portable stove for heat. Customers can choose their favorite fish cakes and other ingredients from a large serving pot, and wash them down with beer or saké while keeping warm around the stove. Outdoor oden stalls are extremely down-to-earth: One oden connoisseur interviewed claimed that it's impossible to find a more informal setting short of actually sitting in the gutter.

If you want to try oden without roughing it, there are also oden specialty shops, and oden can be found at certain other restaurants as well. You can either select your favorite ingredients or order a standard assortment. The individual ingredients include *daikon* (white radish), potatoes, kelp, transparent cakes made from *konnyaku* (devil's-tongue starch), and *fukuro* (fried tofu pouches stuffed with chopped mushrooms and noodles). There are also many different fish cakes, including *chikuwa*, which is made by molding fish paste into a tube shape, steaming it, and finally grilling it. The fish cakes are made from fish that aren't so popular on their own, such as shark, flying fish, and pollack.

Oden is usually served with a dab of strong mustard. People who try oden for the first time often find it a bit bland and they may wonder why it's so popular; oden is something of an acquired taste. Although the flavors tend to be on the subtle side, oden fans also appreciate the unusual and contrasting textures of the different ingredients, as well as

99

the subtle flavor of the broth, which improves with time as it soaks up various flavors.

Oden can be found in specialty oden restaurants, sidewalk stalls, *yakitori* restaurants, and all-purpose pubs. It's usually served in the winter, although it's sometimes available during the warmer months, particularly in specialty oden restaurants.

ODEN MENU

Set Meals

| おでん定食 | *oden teishoku* | oden set meal, with rice, soup, and pickles |
| おでん盛り合わせ | *oden moriawase* | preselected assortment of oden items |

A la Carte Items

はんぺん/半ぺん	*hanpen*	soft white fish cake made with yam
さつま揚げ/薩摩揚げ	*Satsuma-age*	fried fish cakes
ちくわ	*chikuwa*	tube-shaped fish cake
ちくわぶ	*chikuwa-bu*	tube-shaped wheat-gluten cake
つみれ	*tsumire*	fish balls made from sardines or similar fish
ボール(団子)	*bōru (dango)*	fried fish cake in the shape of a ball
すじ	*suji*	steamed fish cake made from shark
ごぼう巻	*gobō-maki*	strips of burdock root wrapped in fish cake
いか	*ika*	squid
いか巻	*ika-maki*	baby squid wrapped in fish cake

げそ巻	*geso-maki*	squid tentacles wrapped in fish cake
たこ(串)	*tako(-gushi)*	octopus (on skewers)
たまご/玉子	*tamago*	hard-boiled eggs
うずら/鶉(玉子)	*uzura tamago*	hard-boiled quail eggs
がんも(どき)	*ganmo(doki)*	fried tofu patties with bits of vegetables
焼豆腐	*yaki-dōfu*	deep-fried tofu
あつ揚げ/厚揚げ	*atsu-age*	fried tofu blocks
ふくろ	*fukuro*	fried tofu bag filled with chopped vegetables
こんにゃく	*konnyaku*	translucent blocks of devil's-tongue starch
しらたき/白たき	*shirataki*	translucent white *konnyaku* noodles
こ(ん)ぶ/昆布	*ko(n)bu*	kelp sheets (rolled up and tied into small knots)
だいこん/大根	*daikon*	Japanese radish
ロールキャベツ	*rōru kyabetsu*	cabbage rolls, wrapped around burdock root or cocktail sausages
ごぼう	*gobō*	burdock root
ウインナー	*uinnā*	cocktail sausage

Okonomiyaki
(Japanese Savory Pancakes)
おこのみやき・お好み焼

Okonomiyaki restaurants (*okonomiyaki-ya*) serve large pancakes made with diced seafood, meat and vegetables. "Okonomiyaki" literally means "cook what you like," and customers get to choose their own favorite ingredients and then cook the tasty pancakes themselves at the table. Because you choose your own ingredients, Japanese often liken okonomiyaki to Western-style pizza, although the similarity is a bit tenuous.

Okonomiyaki-style cooking originated in Osaka, and it continues to be most popular there, although *okonomiyaki-ya* can be found throughout Japan. They're very popular with young people, since the food is tasty, inexpensive, filling, and fun to prepare.

The various main ingredients available will be listed on the menu; an order of okonomiyaki consists of a bowl of pancake-like batter and a dish containing diced vegetables and the main ingredient, such as shrimp or pork. A regular order of shrimp okonomiyaki is called *ebi-ten* (or *ebi-tamayaki*); some restaurants also serve *monja-yaki*, which is a somewhat thinner, more watery pancake.

The waiter or waitress will come by to turn on the grill at your table and brush the surface with oil; after that you're on your own. Start by mixing together all the ingredients, then pour the mixture onto the grill when it's hot enough. You'll find small spatulas with which to flatten the pancake and push it into shape, and a larger spatula with which to turn it over when the time comes. Before and after turning, you can brush the top of the pancake with Worcestershire-flavored sauce, and then sprinkle it with *aonori* (green seaweed powder) and *katsuo* (dried bonito shavings) before eating it.

It takes a bit of experience to figure out when to flip the pancake and when to take it off the grill. Okonomiyaki takes longer to cook than you might expect, and the finished product doesn't hold together near-ly as well as a Western-style pancake. You might ask your waiter for advice, or else pay close attention to the technique of the people at the next table.

Okonomiyaki-ya also serve *yakisoba* (fried Chinese noodles with vegetables), as well as some egg-based dishes that are closer to omelettes than pancakes.

OKONOMIYAKI MENU

Okonomiyaki

一天	*-ten*	okonomiyaki-style (i.e., *ebi-ten*: shrimp okonomiyaki) with ingredients listed below
一玉焼	*-tama-yaki*	okonomiyaki-style (with egg) with ingredients listed below
一もんじゃ焼	*-monja-yaki*	*Shitamachi* (downtown)-style okonomiyaki, slightly thinner than usual, with ingredients listed below
牛	*gyū*	beef
豚	*buta*	pork
とん	*ton*	pork
えび/海老	*ebi*	shrimp
いか	*ika*	squid
やさい/野菜	*yasai*	vegetables
ミックス	*mikkusu*	mixed (some of the ingredients above)
たこ/蛸	*tako*	octopus
ほたて/帆立	*hotate*	scallops
あさり	*asari*	clams
かき/牡蠣	*kaki*	oysters (winter)
なっとう/納豆	*nattō*	sticky, fermented soybeans
コーン	*kōn*	corn
モダン焼	*modan-yaki*	okonomiyaki with fried eggs

| 一焼そば | -yakisoba | fried Chinese noodles (with okonomiyaki ingredients listed above) |

Teppanyaki

鉄板焼	*teppanyaki*	grilled foods
一バター焼	*-batā-yaki*	foods grilled in butter (some okonomiyaki items listed above, plus those listed below)
じゃが(いも)	*jaga(imo)*	potato
とうふ/豆腐	*tōfu*	bean curd
なす/茄子	*nasu*	eggplant
しいたけ/椎茸	*shiitake*	Japanese mushrooms
えのき	*enoki*	slender white mushrooms
げそ/下足	*geso*	squid tentacles
いか丸焼き	*ika maru-yaki*	whole grilled squid

Table Condiments

青のり/青海苔	*aonori*	dried seaweed powder
かつおぶし/鰹節	*katsuo-bushi*	dried bonito flakes
ソース	*sōsu*	Worcestershire-like sauce
甘ロー	*amakuchi-*	sweet sauce
辛ロー	*karakuchi-*	slightly spicy sauce
しょうゆ	*shōyu*	soy sauce
(紅)しょうが/生姜	*(beni) shōga*	pickled ginger (dyed red)

Useful Phrases

Please turn (up/down) the flame.
Hi o (tsuyoku/yowaku) shite kudasai.
火を(強く/弱く)してください。

Please turn off the burner.   *Hi o tomete kudasai.* 火を止めてください。

Do you think this is done yet?
Mō taberaremasu ka?　もう食べられますか?

Yes.   *Hai, (taberaremasu).*　はい、(食べられます)。

Not yet.   *Iie./Mada.*　いいえ/まだ。

Teppanyaki (Grilled Steaks)
てっぱん焼・鉄板焼

Japanese steak houses (also known as *teppanyaki-ya*) present a good example of the elaborate preparation and careful, artistic presentation that typify much of Japanese cuisine. Although a steak dinner would seem like one of the simplest meals in the world to prepare, teppanyaki chefs turn it into a spectacle, with knives and spatulas flashing at lightning speed, and tender slices of steak and vegetables sizzling dramatically at your table. This cooking method is a fairly recent innovation in Japan, and part of the appeal of teppanyaki restaurants is the novelty and entertainment value of the preparation. The other drawing factor is, of course, the food itself, which may include tender Kobe beef, fresh forest mushrooms and snow peas, and even prawns and scallops, all seasoned gently and grilled to perfection.

Since beef is a luxury item in Japan, and since teppanyaki restaurants are often used for business entertaining, the prices tend to be on the expensive side. The decor and atmosphere is usually Western rather than Japanese, and generally wine is served rather than saké. Often teppanyaki restaurants have a bar as well.

Steaks are ordered by weight, with 225 grams roughly equivalent to half a pound. If you're not in the mood for beef, grilled chicken, pork, shrimp, and lobster are also available, as are *shiitake* mushrooms and other vegetables. Steaks may be ordered rare, medium, or well-done, and you may specify regular grilling, *batā-yaki* (grilled in butter), or *sherī-yaki* (cooked with sherry sauce).

TEPPANYAKI MENU

Steaks

-鉄板焼	*-teppanyaki*	grilled

一バター焼	*-batā yaki*	grilled in butter
一シェリー焼	*-sherī yaki*	grilled with sherry
サーロインステーキ	*sāroin sutēki*	sirloin steak
ヒレステーキ	*hire sutēki*	fillet steak
テンダーロイン ステーキ	*tendāroin sutēki*	tenderloin steak
和風ステーキ	*wafū sutēki*	Japanese-style steak, with *miso* (soybean paste)
もろみステーキ	*moromi sutēki*	steak with sweet *miso*
子牛鉄板焼	*ko-ushi teppanyaki*	grilled veal
ミックスグリル	*mikkusu guriru*	mixed grill
一コース	*-kōsu*	''course meal'' (steak and other grilled foods)

A la Carte Items

くるま海老/車海老	*kuruma-ebi*	prawn
えび/海老	*ebi*	shrimp
ほたて貝/帆立貝	*hotategai*	scallops
いか	*ika*	squid
(季節の)野菜 盛り合わせ	*(kisetsu no) yasai moriawase*	(seasonal) mixed vegetables
生椎茸	*nama-shiitake*	fresh *shiitake* mushrooms
きのこ/木の子	*kinoko*	mushrooms (a generic term)
ピーマン	*pīman*	green pepper
ししとう	*shishitō*	small Japanese green pepper
サラダ	*sarada*	salad
ワイン	*wain*	wine
赤ワイン	*aka wain*	red wine
白ワイン	*shiro wain*	white wine

Izakaya (Pubs)
居酒屋

The word "*izakaya*" refers to a wide range of pub-style restaurants ranging from very large, noisy places crowded with college students to smaller noisy places that cater to a neighborhood crowd. What they all have in common is an extensive variety of foods (both Japanese and Western-style), inexpensive drinks, and a very casual atmosphere. They provide a comfortable place where you can sit and relax with friends, and where you can enjoy anything from a quick snack to an inexpensive evening's entertainment.

Small neighborhood izakaya often display large red lanterns, called *aka-chōchin*. This custom is so prevalent that the name "*aka-chōchin*" has come to refer not only to the lanterns but to the pubs themselves. Larger izakaya, many of which are popular with students or younger office workers, can be recognized by their enormous size (by Japanese restaurant standards) and by their displays of beer and whiskey next to the food models in the display window. Some traditional izakaya can be identified by the large statues of badgers outside the door.

The atmosphere inside is very relaxed, fun, and usually a bit noisy. The waiters and waitresses wear traditional Japanese clothing, and they're constantly shouting out food orders and enthusiastically greeting new customers. When they're not shouting you can hear the Japanese music being played in the background; izakaya are among the few restaurants where you can catch up on the latest Japanese pop songs. The larger pubs attract fairly large groups, and some of them have special rooms set aside for office parties or college gatherings.

Since pubs are oriented toward drinking, you're usually expected to order a beverage, although of course soft drinks are available in addition to beer and whiskey. Everyone is brought an *otsumami* (or *tsukidashi*), a tiny appetizer to go along with his drink (although it's usually given only to those who order alcoholic drinks, so don't be surprised if you don't get one when you order a Coke). Another custom is for each person at the table to order at least one food item from the menu. There's always a profusion of small, inexpensive side dishes, so you can order lots of different dishes if you're hungry. They cover a wide spectrum of Japanese foods, including *sashimi* (raw fish platter), grilled fish, *yakitori* (grilled chicken), and *nabemono*-style stews. Other, smaller dishes that are served mainly in pubs include *nikujaga* (a meat and potato stew) and certain tofu specialties. Western-style dishes such as salads, baked potatoes, french fries, miniature pizzas, and sausages are also available.

After you've ordered a round of food you can tell the waiter: "*Toriaezu*" ("That's all for now"). If you get hungry after another couple of beers, you can always order a few more snacks without worrying about straining your budget.

In the summertime, large department stores operate open-air "beer gardens" on their roofs. Beer gardens have much the same feeling as regular pubs, only they're out under the stars. They serve a menu similar to that of pubs, but the selection is a bit more limited and the prices are slightly higher.

The sample menu in this section covers some of the most common dishes found in both izakaya and *robatayaki* restaurants (described on page 114). You may also refer to the menus in the chapters on *yakitori*, *kushiage*, *nabemono*, etc., and the list of seafood names in the sushi chapter. Some izakaya specialize in one particular style of cooking or in a regional cuisine, while others are more generalized. For more information on drinking customs, refer to the chapter "**Drinking in Japan**" (page 154).

IZAKAYA AND ROBATAYAKI MENU

Sashimi (Raw Fish) and Sunomono (Vinegared Dishes)

Note: Refer also to the "**Sushi Menu**," page 56.

刺身盛り合わせ	*sashimi moriawase*	platter of assorted raw fish
（お）造り	*(o)tsukuri*	same as *sashimi moriawase*
‒刺	*-sashi*	raw fish

–たたき/叩き	*-tataki*	pounded, very slightly cooked fish
–酢	*-su*	vinegared dish
いわし/鰯	*iwashi*	sardine
あまえび/甘海老	*ama-ebi*	raw shrimp
あじ/鯵	*aji*	horse mackerel
はまち	*hamachi*	young yellowtail
まぐろ/鮪	*maguro*	tuna
いか	*ika*	squid
しらすおろし	*shirasu oroshi*	baby sardines served with grated radish
なめこおろし	*nameko oroshi*	tiny mushrooms and grated radish
とり刺し	*tori-sashi*	raw chicken platter
(まぐろ)山かけ	*(maguro) yamakake*	raw tuna topped with grated yam
たこ酢/蛸酢	*tako su*	vinegared boiled octopus
ほや酢	*hoya su*	vinegared sea squirt
なまこ酢	*namako su*	vinegared sea cucumber
わかめ酢	*wakame su*	vinegared seaweed (strips)
もずく酢	*mozuku su*	vinegared seaweed (strands)
めんたいこ/明太子	*mentaiko*	spicy cod roe
しおから/塩辛	*shiokara*	salted squid intestines

Yakimono (Grilled Foods)

COOKING STYLES:

–焼	*-yaki*	grilled
–串焼	*-kushi-yaki*	grilled on skewers
–バター焼	*-batā-yaki*	grilled in butter
–塩焼	*-shio-yaki*	grilled with salt
–梅焼	*-ume-yaki*	grilled with Japanese plum sauce
–つぼ焼	*-tsubo-yaki*	shellfish cooked in their shells
–てり焼/ 照り焼	*-teri-yaki*	grilled and basted with soy sauce and sweetened cooking saké

−石焼	*-ishi-yaki*	grilled over hot stones
−ほうろく焼	*-hōroku-yaki*	cooked with salt in a covered earthenware dish
−いそ(べ)焼/ 磯(辺)焼	*-iso(be)-yaki*	("shore grill") grilled skewered seafood
御狩場焼	*okariba-yaki*	("hunter's grill") game birds and vegetables grilled in butter or oil

INGREDIENTS:

ししゃも	*shishamo*	smelt
えいひれ	*eihire*	ray fillet
さんま/秋刀魚	*sanma*	mackerel pike; saury
にしん/鰊	*nishin*	herring
ほっけ	*hokke*	Atka mackerel
さけ/鮭	*sake*	salmon
あじ/鰺	*aji*	horse mackerel
えび/海老	*ebi*	shrimp
くるま海老/ 車海老	*kuruma-ebi*	prawns
焼はまぐり/ 焼蛤	*yaki hamaguri*	grilled clams
ほたて貝/帆立貝	*hotategai*	scallops
(いか)げそ/下足	*(ika) geso*	squid tentacles
いか(丸焼)	*ika (maru-yaki)*	squid (whole; grilled)
かれい	*karei*	flounder
するめ	*surume*	dried cuttlefish (in strips)
あさり	*asari*	short-necked clams
くじら/鯨	*kujira*	whale
手羽先	*tebasaki*	chicken wings
つくね	*tsukune*	chicken meatballs
やきとり/焼鳥	*yakitori*	broiled chicken (on skewers)
ささみ	*sasami*	boneless chicken breast
じゃがいもバター	*jagaimo batā*	potato fried in butter (also called *jaga-batā*)
しいたけ/椎茸	*shiitake*	mushrooms

しめじ	shimeji	slender mushrooms
なす焼き/ 茄子焼き	nasu yaki	grilled eggplant
ピーマン	pīman	green pepper
ししとう	shishitō	small Japanese green pepper
アスパラベーコン	asupara bēkon	asparagus wrapped in bacon
にんにく	ninniku	garlic
えのき	enoki	thin white mushrooms
はんぺん/半ぺん	hanpen	a soft cake made of white fish and grated yam
あつ揚げ/厚揚げ	atsu-age	deep-fried tofu blocks
でんがく/田楽	dengaku	tofu and/or devil's-tongue block broiled with slightly sweetened *miso* (soybean paste)
なす田楽	nasu dengaku	eggplant broiled with slightly sweetened *miso* paste
豆腐ステーキ	tōfu sutēki	broiled tofu steak with soy sauce and grated radish dip

Agemono (Fried Foods)

ポテトフライ	poteto furai	fried potatoes; french fries
(若)鳥から揚げ	(waka)tori kara-age	(young) chicken deep-fried without batter
げそから揚げ	geso kara-age	squid tentacles deep-fried without batter
揚げ出し(豆腐)	agedashi(-dōfu)	fried tofu served with grated radish and soy sauce
かわえび/川海老	kawa-ebi	small fried freshwater shrimps
チーズ(包み)揚げ	chīzu (tsutsumi)-age	fried cheese rolls
なすチーズ揚げ	nasu chīzu age	eggplant and cheese

Otsumami (Snacks) and Nimono (Stewed Foods)

| えだまめ/枝豆 | edamame | green soybeans served in their shells as a snack |

冷奴	*hiya yakko*	cold tofu blocks garnished with grated ginger, chopped scallions, and soy sauce
冷しトマト	*hiyashi tomato*	cold sliced tomatoes
(御)新香	*(o)shinko*	Japanese pickled vegetables
ぎんなん/銀杏	*ginnan*	ginkgo nuts
もろきゅう	*morokyū*	cucumber sticks served with *miso* (soybean paste)
梅きゅうり	*umekyūri*	cucumber sticks served with Japanese *ume* plum
なっとう/納豆	*nattō*	fermented soybeans (an acquired taste)
板わさ	*itawasa*	sliced fish cake served with Japanese horseradish
しゅうまい/ シュウマイ	*shūmai*	steamed Chinese-style pork dumplings
バターコーン	*batā kōn*	grilled corn with butter
ソーセージ	*sōsēji*	sausages
肉じゃが	*nikujaga*	potatoes stewed with bits of pork
煮込み	*nikomi*	stewed vegetables, sometimes with meat or giblets
肉豆腐	*niku-dōfu*	tofu simmered with bits of pork
茶わん蒸し	*chawan mushi*	steamed egg custard with bits of vegetables, seafood, and chicken
きんぴら	*kinpira*	carrots and burdock root lightly sautéed in sesame oil and seasoned with soy sauce and red pepper
おでん	*oden*	assorted fish cakes, radish chunks, and other vegetables simmered in kelp-flavored stock
あら煮	*arani*	stewed fish
みそ汁/味噌汁	*miso shiru*	soybean-paste soup

Salads

和風サラダ	*wafū sarada*	Japanese-style salad with sesame-and-vinegar dressing
中華サラダ	*chūka sarada*	salad with spicy Chinese-style dressing and/or Chinese vegetables
海草サラダ	*kaisō sarada*	seaweed salad
わかめサラダ	*wakame sarada*	seaweed salad
ツナサラダ	*tsuna sarada*	tuna salad
生野菜	*nama yasai*	a combination plate of assorted raw vegetables, usually served with a soy-based vinaigrette

Rice and Noodle Dishes

おにぎり	*onigiri*	rice balls wrapped in *nori* (dried seaweed)
焼おにぎり	*yaki-onigiri*	roasted rice balls, usually without *nori*
茶づけ/茶漬	*chazuke*	white rice covered with green tea or fish broth
うめ/梅–	*ume-*	*chazuke* with a Japanese pickled plum (*ume*) at the bottom
のり/海苔–	*nori-*	*chazuke* topped with *nori* (dried seaweed) strips
さけ/鮭–	*sake-*	*chazuke* with a piece of salmon at the bottom
めんたいこ–/明太子–	*mentaiko-*	*chazuke* with spiced cod roe at the bottom
かに雑炊	*kani zōsui*	crabmeat-flavored rice soup
玉子雑炊	*tamago zōsui*	rice soup with egg
やきそば/焼そば	*yakisoba*	fried Chinese-style noodles
焼うどん	*yakiudon*	fried *udon* wheat noodles

Robatayaki (Japanese Barbecue)
ろばた焼・炉端焼

Robatayaki-style pubs are similar to regular Japanese pubs (*izakaya*) in that they serve a wide variety of foods as well as drinks. They specialize, though, in charcoal-grilled delicacies, ranging from grilled fish and meats to tofu and vegetables.

The name *robatayaki* means "hearthside cooking," and robatayaki restaurants strive to recreate the warm atmosphere of traditional Japanese country farmhouses. These farmhouses always featured a large square fireplace, located in the center of the room and used for both cooking and general heating. The fireplace would serve as a focal point for the daily activities on the farm, especially during the winter months. Robatayaki restaurants are decorated in a similarly rustic manner, with rough wooden beams and stone floors, and farm tools used as wall decorations. Instead of a fireplace they feature open charcoal grills where the customers can watch their food being broiled. Smaller robatayaki may have a counter arrangement instead of open grills, but the decor is just as countrified.

The menus at robatayaki restaurants are as varied as those at regular pubs, ranging from *yakitori* chicken and skewered *kushiage* to *sashimi* platters. Many varieties of *yaki-zakana* (grilled fish) are featured, and you may also find foods that use special charcoal-grill cooking techniques, such as teriyaki (fish or chicken basted with soy sauce and rice wine) or *karayaki* (shellfish baked in their own shells). Other dishes may include *yaki-onigiri* (roasted rice balls) and grilled mushrooms, ginkgo nuts, eggplants, and potatoes.

For ordering in robatayaki restaurants, refer to the sample menu in the "**Izakaya**" chapter (page 108), paying particular attention to the section on *yakimono* (grilled foods).

Regional Specialties
地方料理・郷土料理

Tokyo is the cultural, political, and business center of Japan, and people from every part of the country are drawn to it. When they occasionally get homesick, they can escape the hustle and bustle of the big city by visiting a restaurant or pub specializing in the cuisine of their home region. Regional cooking tends to be country-style cooking, featuring the fresh produce and seafood indigenous to the region.

Regional restaurants in Tokyo (and a few other major cities) strive to recreate both the cuisine and the atmosphere of the areas they represent, often flying in fresh native ingredients.

The usual way to discover a regional restaurant is to hear about it from friends or to read about it in a guidebook. Occasionally, however, you can recognize one by its countrified look or by the presence of certain rustic decorations, such as a waterwheel, a bear with a salmon in its mouth, or a stone pathway. Usually the name of the region (in Japanese characters) will appear somewhere on the sign (see menu section below), or you can ask inside (see page 45).

Japanese cooking varies greatly from place to place, in both ingredients and cooking styles. Hokkaido, the northernmost and coldest island, is known for its salmon and herring dishes, including many *nabemono* dishes (hotpot-style stews). Kagoshima, at the opposite end of Japan, is situated at the southern end of the island of Kyushu, and Kagoshima cuisine is known for its delicious pork stews. Other regions in between have their own noteworthy foods and dishes, such as the rice and saké from Akita Prefecture, the tofu dishes of Kyoto, and the special *wanko-soba* of Iwate Prefecture, which is served in tiny refillable dishes with a myriad of rich toppings.

In addition to the country-style regional dishes, there are also more sophisticated specialties from Japan's urban regions. For example, traditional Tokyo-style cuisine includes *nigiri-zushi* and *kabayaki*-style eel. Kyoto, once Japan's capital, was the original home of the elegant *kaiseki*-style service, which is described in the "**Nihon-ryōri**" chapter. And Nagasaki, on the western coast of Kyushu, was for centuries Japan's only trading post with the outside world, and its cuisine reflects that fact by featuring dishes with strong Chinese and European influences.

There's such a wide variety of regional specialty dishes that it would be difficult to list them all here. Most regional restaurants serve a mix of special local dishes and standard Japanese dishes, although often even the standard dishes vary in preparation and flavoring. The sample menu below describes some popular regional specialties, while the menu in the "**Izakaya**" chapter lists some standard Japanese dishes that are available. (Other dishes are listed in the "**Japanese Food Vocabulary**" section.) You can also ask the waiter to recommend the specialties of the house.

REGIONAL MENU

Regions of Japan

北海道	*Hokkaidō*	the northernmost of Japan's four main islands, famous for its cold winters and its salmon, other fish, and dairy products
東北	*Tōhoku*	the northern part of Japan's main island, Honshu, known for its fish, rice, and *nabemono* (quick-cooked stews)
関東	*Kantō*	the eastern part of Honshu, including Tokyo
関西	*Kansai*	the western part of Honshu, including Osaka and Kyoto
京都	*Kyōto*	the former capital of Japan, where *kaiseki-ryōri* (tea-ceremony cuisine) and *shōjin-ryōri* (vegetarian temple cuisine) originated. Also known for its tofu. (*See also* "**Nihon-ryōri**," page 120.)

広島	*Hiroshima*	on the far western tip of Honshu, known for its oysters and fish
四国	*Shikoku*	the smallest of Japan's major islands, with a warm climate and many fishing ports
九州	*Kyūshū*	the southernmost major island, with a climate ranging from warm to semi-tropical
長崎	*Nagasaki*	on the western coast of Kyushu, Nagasaki enjoys a cuisine that is heavily influenced by both Chinese and Western cuisines
鹿児島	*Kagoshima*	the southernmost part of Kyushu, well known for its saké and its pork dishes
沖縄	*Okinawa*	a semi-tropical island south of the major Japanese islands, near Taiwan

Some Regional Specialty Dishes and Foods

HOKKAIDO:

| いしかり鍋/石狩鍋 | *ishikari-nabe* | *nabemono* (quick-cooked stew) made with salmon, salmon roe, *miso* (soybean paste), and vegetables |
| るいべ | *ruibe* | partially frozen raw whale or salmon sashimi |

TŌHOKU:

| しょっつる鍋 | *shottsuru-nabe* | (western Tōhoku, esp. Akita Prefecture) *nabemono* made with Japanese-style fish sauce (similar to Thai fish sauce) and vegetables |
| わんこそば | *wanko-soba* | (eastern Tōhoku, esp. Iwate Prefecture) *soba* served in tiny bowls with various toppings |

TOKYO:

| おでん | *oden* | fish cakes and vegetables simmered in broth (see page 99) |

KANTO:

じぶ煮	jibuni	(northern Kanto) chicken and vegetables stewed in soy sauce, sweetened saké, and stock
けぬき寿司	kenuki-zushi	(western Kanto) rice and raw fish wrapped in bamboo leaves

KYOTO:

甘鯛の西京漬	amadai no saikyōzuke	tilefish marinated in *miso* (soybean paste) and grilled
はも	hamo	conger eel which is charcoal-grilled or boiled
なまふ	namafu	wheat gluten cakes, which are served in a variety of styles and flavors in vegetarian temple cuisine
たけのこ	takenoko	bamboo shoots, also served in a variety of styles
とり鍋/鳥鍋	tori-nabe	(Nara, near Kyoto) *nabemono* made with chicken and vegetables

KANSAI:

バッテラ(鮨)	battera(-zushi)	cooked, marinated fish on blocks of rice
ふな鮨/鮒鮨	funazushi	lightly aged, pickled raw fish
かも鍋/鴨鍋	kamo-nabe	(western Kansai) *nabemono* made with wild duck and vegetables
ぼたん鍋/牡丹鍋	botan-nabe	*nabemono* made with wild boar

HIROSHIMA:

どて鍋/土手鍋	dote-nabe	*nabemono* made with oysters and vegetables and flavored with *miso*
ままかり漬	mamakari-zuke	(Okayama, near Hiroshima) herrings pickled in vinegar and ginger

KYUSHU:

チャンポン	chanpon	(Nagasaki) Chinese *rāmen* noodles and chopped vegetables in soup
しゅうへい鍋	shūhei-nabe	(Nagasaki) *nabemono* made with fish and pounded rice cakes
とんこつ/豚骨	tonkotsu	(southern Kyushu, esp. Kagoshima) pork (with bones) stewed slowly in *miso* and *shōchū* (distilled liquor)
ふぐ/河豚	fugu	blowfish (*see* page 64)
さか鮨/酒鮨	saka-zushi	sushi made with saké instead of vinegar

Nihon-Ryōri
(General Japanese Cuisine)
日本料理・和風

Although most restaurants in Japan are easily classifiable according to type of food or cooking style, some places are harder to pigeonhole. They serve a wide variety of different Japanese foods, and often cultivate a traditional Japanese atmosphere through their music, decor, and the garb of the waiters and waitresses.

Kaiseki restaurants are the most elaborate and expensive of these. A *kaiseki* meal is made up of many small delicacies carefully selected to reflect the season and to counterbalance each other in taste, texture, color, and method of cooking. *Kaiseki* cuisine has its origins in the traditional tea ceremony practiced in certain Buddhist temples in Kyoto in the 1700s. Even today traditional *kaiseki* cuisine uses no meat, in keeping with strict Buddhist practice. *Kaiseki* restaurants tend to be hard to find, and are rather discreet in their decor. There is usually a fixed meal or a choice of a few different fixed meals with different prices.

Ryōtei serve less formal and elaborate meals than *kaiseki* restaurants. They feature one or more chefs who are skilled in various Japanese cooking styles. Some *ryōtei* resemble ordinary restaurants, while others are very discreet and seem more like private clubs. These private *ryōtei* tend to be expensive, and may require an introduction from a regular patron. Smaller *ryōtei* are sometimes called **kappō** restaurants, while Japanese-style inns that feature food are called **ryokan**. Many *ryokan* are renowned for their excellent meals.

Places specializing in Kyoto-style cuisine are called **Kyō-fū** or **Kyō-ryōri** restaurants, or **Kyō-kaiseki** if they're more formal. Kyoto-style cuisine is much more sophisticated than other regional cuisines, which tend to favor country-style recipes. Since Kyoto is landlocked, its chefs were forced to develop elaborate methods of food preparation to make up for their lack of fresh ingredients. For example, a multitude of inventive techniques for preparing tofu, a staple of the Buddhist religious diet, were developed in Kyoto. In fact, much of traditional Japanese cuisine originated in Kyoto, and many of the best eateries in Tokyo are branches of restaurants that started in Kyoto or nearby Osaka.

Less fancy than *ryōtei*, ordinary **wafū** (Japanese-style) restaurants can be found on department-store restaurant floors and other places. They feature traditional Japanese *koto* music, kimono-clad waitresses, and a variety of ordinary Japanese dishes, such as tempura, sushi, *kamameshi*, and so forth, usually arranged in set meals.

Shokudō are very inexpensive general-purpose restaurants and cafeterias serving a wide variety of foods. These may include so-called Western-style foods such as pork fried in ginger, deep-fried shrimps, and "hamburger" steaks with pickles and rice. **Yō-shoku** ("Western-style") restaurants specialize exclusively in these dishes.

Kaiseki and other expensive restaurants usually have a set meal or a few set meals in different price ranges, which greatly simplifies the problems of ordering. In ordinary Japanese-style restaurants, there may be a wide selection of course meals that are given poetic names (flowers, snow, moon, etc.); refer to the section **"Numbers and Basic Menu Vocabulary"** on page 45 for help in reading these names.

The menu section below lists a number of common dishes that are served in general Japanese-style restaurants. For items not listed, you may also refer to the **"Japanese Food Vocabulary"** section on page 161, the **"Izakaya/Robatayaki Menu"** on page 108, and the other specialty menus in this book.

NIHON-RYŌRI MENU

Suimono (Soups)

（お）すまし	*(o)sumashi*	clear soups
まつたけ/松茸	*matsutake*	Japanese pine mushroom
海老（しんじょ）	*ebi (shinjo)*	(diced) shrimp
はまぐり/蛤	*hamaguri*	clam (also called *ushio-jiru*)

みそ汁/味噌汁	*miso shiru*	soups with *miso* soy paste
赤だし	*akadashi*	red *miso* paste
豆腐	*tōfu*	bean curd
なめこ	*nameko*	tiny mushrooms
しじみ	*shijimi*	small clams

Mushimono (Steamed Dishes)

茶わん蒸し/茶碗蒸し	*chawan-mushi*	egg custard with bits of vegetables and chicken (not sweet; served hot)
かぶら蒸し	*kabura-mushi*	steamed fish with turnips and egg white
ちり蒸し	*chiri-mushi*	steamed fish custard
玉子豆腐	*tamago-dōfu*	cold egg custard with the consistency of tofu (not sweet; served cold)
ごま豆腐/胡麻豆腐	*goma-dōfu*	a tofu-like food made of powdered arrowroot and flavored with sesame

Sashimi (Raw Fish and Other Foods)

Note: Refer also to the "**Sushi Menu**," page 56.

刺身盛り合わせ	*sashimi moriawase*	raw fish assortment platter
たい(鯛)の刺身	*tai no sashimi*	raw sea bream
すずきの刺身	*suzuki no sashimi*	raw sea bass
ますの刺身	*masu no sashimi*	raw trout
あわびの刺身	*awabi no sashimi*	raw abalone
(お)造り	*(o)tsukuri*	*sashimi* arranged on a platter
うす造り	*usuzukuri*	raw fish sliced paper-thin
糸造り	*itozukuri*	raw fish sliced in thin, string-like strips
(こい/鯉)あらい	*(koi) arai*	thinly sliced (carp) artfully arranged on a bed of ice
かつお/鰹 たたき/叩き	*katsuo tataki*	bonito pounded and served mostly raw, after being broiled but a few moments

あじたたき	*aji tataki*	horse mackerel *tataki*
牛たたき	*gyū tataki*	beef *tataki*
るいべ	*ruibe*	partially frozen raw salmon or whale
馬刺	*basashi*	raw horsemeat (also called *sakura-niku*)

Yakimono (Broiled Dishes)

Note: Refer also to the *yakimono* section of the "**Izakaya/Robatayaki Menu**" on page 109.

やきとり/焼鳥	*yakitori*	grilled chicken on skewers (*see also* "**Yakitori Menu**," page 85)
塩焼	*shio-yaki*	fish grilled with salt
つぼ焼	*tsubo-yaki*	shellfish cooked in their shells
（豆腐）田楽	*(tōfu) dengaku*	(bean curd) grilled with *miso* soybean paste
なす田楽	*nasu dengaku*	eggplant *dengaku*
ほうろく焼	*hōroku-yaki*	food baked with salt in a covered earthenware dish
包み焼	*tsutsumi-yaki*	fish wrapped in foil or paper and grilled
ほうしょ焼	*hōsho yaki*	fish (or other food) wrapped in paper and grilled
玉子焼	*tamago yaki*	sweetened, firm, lightly fried egg
-西京漬	*-saikyōzuke*	-marinated in *miso* soybean paste and grilled (Kansai-style)
（海老）黄身焼	*(ebi) kimiyaki*	(shrimp) coated with egg yolk and grilled
（いか）うに焼	*(ika) uniyaki*	(squid) coated with sea urchin roe and grilled

Nimono (Stewed Dishes)

| さかなの煮つけ | *sakana no nitsuke* | fish stewed in soy sauce and sweet saké |

煮ざかな	*nizakana*	stewed fish
(かれいの)煮つけ	*(karei no) nitsuke*	stewed (flounder)
鯛のかぶと煮	*tai no kabuto-ni*	stewed head ("helmet") of sea bream
みがきにしん	*migaki nishin*	stewed dried herring
たこの桜煮	*tako no sakurani*	stewed octopus
肉の煮物	*niku no nimono*	stewed meat dishes
豚の角煮	*buta no kakuni*	stewed fatty pork
鳥の筑前煮	*tori no chikuzen-ni*	(Kyushu-style) stewed chicken
肉じゃが	*niku jaga*	stewed beef with potatoes
野菜の煮物	*yasai no nimono*	stewed vegetables
旬の煮物 (盛り合わせ)	*shun no nimono* *(moriawase)*	assortment of stewed seasonal vegetables (such as okra, eggplant, and squash)
季節の炊き合わせ (煮物)	*kisetsu no takiawase*	same as *shun no nimono* (Osaka area)
ふろふき(大根)	*furofuki (daikon)*	stewed Japanese radish

Agemono (Fried Dishes)

てんぷら/天婦羅	*tempura*	lightly battered, deep-fried seafood and vegetables (see "**Tempura Menu**," page 68)
串揚	*kushiage*	thick-crusted, deep-fried seafood and vegetables on skewers
(鳥)から揚げ/ 唐揚げ	*(tori) kara-age*	(chicken) deep-fried without batter
かれいのから揚げ	*karei no kara-age*	flounder *kara-age*
(若鳥)たつた揚げ/ 竜田揚げ	*(wakadori)* *tatsuta-age*	(young chicken) marinated, then deep-fried
あげだし豆腐/ 揚げ出し豆腐	*agedashi dōfu*	deep-fried bean curd served with dried bonito flakes, a soy-based broth, and grated radish

Nabemono (Quick-Cooked Stews)

Note: Refer also to the "**Nabemono Menu**," page 93.

すきやき/好き焼き	*sukiyaki*	thinly sliced beef and vegetables
しゃぶしゃぶ	*shabu-shabu*	very thinly sliced beef (see "**Sukiyaki and Shabu-Shabu Menu**," page 97)
ちり鍋	*chiri-nabe*	fish-and-vegetable stew
(かきの)どて鍋/土手鍋	*(kaki no) doté-nabe*	oyster-and-vegetable stew with *miso* soybean paste
水炊き	*mizutaki*	chicken-and-vegetable stew
やながわ鍋/柳川鍋	*yanagawa-nabe*	stew of loach (a small, eel-like fish), burdock root, and egg

Aemono (Dishes Dressed with Sauces)

酢の物	*sunomono*	vinegared dishes
かに酢	*kanizu*	vinegared crabmeat
酢だこ	*sudako*	octopus in vinegar sauce
(まぐろ)ぬた	*(maguro) nuta*	(tuna) with vinegar, tiny scallions, and *miso* paste
いかぬた	*ika nuta*	squid *nuta*
ほうれん草の胡麻あえ	*hōrensō no goma-ae*	boiled spinach with sesame-soy dressing
(和風)サラダ	*(wafū) sarada*	salad (with Japanese-style soy dressing)

Otsumami (Hors d'Oeuvres)

Note: Refer also to the *otsumami* section in the "**Izakaya/Robatayaki Menu**" on page 111.

おつまみ	*otsumami*	snacks to be eaten while drinking
(いかの)しおから/塩辛	*(ika no) shiokara*	salted (squid) intestines
(まぐろ)山かけ	*(maguro) yamakake*	tuna dressed with foamy grated yam

(なめこ)おろし	*(nameko) oroshi*	(tiny mushrooms) dressed with grated radish
生うに	*nama uni*	raw sea-urchin roe
枝豆	*edamame*	boiled green soybeans (served in the pod)
冷奴	*hiya yakko*	tofu cubes served in cold water

Gohan-mono (Rice Dishes)

鯛めし	*tai-meshi*	rice with sea bream
五目めし	*gomoku meshi*	rice with chicken, fried tofu, and vegetables
釜めし	*kamameshi*	rice steamed with various ingredients (*see* "**Kamameshi Menu**," page 90)
栗ごはん	*kuri gohan*	rice with chestnuts
赤飯	*sekihan*	glutinous rice cooked with red *azuki* beans
(梅)茶づけ/茶漬	*(ume) chazuke*	rice in a bowl of green tea (with pickled Japanese plum)
おにぎり	*onigiri*	rice balls wrapped in dried seaweed
焼むすび	*yaki musubi*	roasted rice balls
(かに)雑炊	*(kani) zōsui*	rice soup (with crabmeat)
(天)丼	*(ten)don*	(tempura-fried prawn) over rice
(うな)重	*(una)jū*	(grilled eel) served over rice in a rectangular box

Menrui (Noodles)

Note: Refer also to the "**Soba Menu**," page 73.

| もり/盛(そば) | *mori (soba)* | *soba* noodles piled on a bamboo screen |
| (天)せいろ | *(ten-)seiro* | *mori soba* (topped with tempura-fried prawns) |

| ざる（そば） | *zaru (soba)* | *mori soba* topped with dried seaweed strips |
| 茶そば | *chasoba* | *soba* noodles made with green-tea powder |

Set Meals

Note: Moderately priced Japanese restaurants (including many in department stores) often have set meals with poetic names ("bamboo set," "chrysanthemum set," etc.); these names are described in the chapter entitled "**Reading Numbers and Basic Vocabulary Terms**" on page 45.

弁当	*bentō*	boxed lunch
幕の内弁当	*makunouchi bentō*	"special of the house" boxed lunch
手さげ弁当	*tesage bentō*	a boxed lunch served in a basket
和定食	*wa teishoku*	Japanese-style set meal
–定食	*-teishoku*	set meal (with rice, pickles, and soup)
–(御)膳	*-(go)zen*	a more elaborate set meal, with several different dishes

Yakiniku (Korean Barbecue)
やきにく・焼肉

Koreans make up the second-largest ethnic group in Japan (after the Japanese), and this demographic fact is reflected in the abundance of fairly authentic Korean barbecue restaurants. Korean-style barbecue is known in Japanese simply as *yakiniku* (lit. "roasted meat"), but the main specialty is always a tasty marinated grilled beef. Customers barbecue the beef right at the table, and the fats and marinating juices drip onto the grill to produce billows of aromatic smoke, which flavor the meat as it cooks. The barbecued beef is usually accompanied by white rice and spicy *kim chee* (Korean-style pickles).

Yakiniku restaurants can be recognized by the characters for "*yakiniku*" (焼肉), although sometimes the sign will say "Korean Barbecue" in English. Inside, there are tables for four to six people, each with a built-in grill and an overhead ventilating chimney. Newer yakiniku restaurants sometimes use specially designed grills with ventilating fans built right into the tables, which keep the smoke from pervading the room. The built-in fans tend to work much better than the overhead chimneys, which leave a lot of smoke in the air. So if smoke bothers you for whatever reason, or if you don't want your clothes to smell like a Korean barbecue restaurant, you might want to peek inside to check what kind of ventilating system is being used and whether or not it seems to be working properly.

Two different types of beef are available, *rōsu*, which is sliced, marinated lean beef, and *karubi*, marinated beef from the ribs. Each type may come in regular- and large-size portions. Since beef is expensive in Japan, the regular portion may seem a bit small, so you might want to order a large size if you're hungry. Assorted vegetables (mushrooms, pumpkin, green peppers, etc.) make a nice side dish when grilled alongside the meat. *Kim chee* (Korean-style pickled cabbage, which is laced with garlic and red peppers) is another tasty side dish that's highly recommended. Besides ordinary beef, other meats such as tongue and liver may also be grilled, and adventurous eaters may be interested in the exotic-sounding Korean stews and rice dishes found on some menus. If you're a yakiniku novice, though, I highly recommend the grilled *rōsu* for your first experience.

After you've ordered, the waiter will light your grill, then bring all the ingredients on big platters. Add the meat and vegetables to the grill a few pieces at a time, and remove them when they're done. Vegetables like pumpkin and onions take a lot longer to cook than the meat, but don't forget to take them off before they burn. You'll find a tiny dish of sauce to dip your meat into after cooking, or you may just find a small empty dish into which you can add one of the two sauces, sweet and spicy, that are usually on each table. If you need to adjust or turn off the flame, you can ask the waiter (see phrase section below) or do it yourself.

YAKINIKU MENU

Korean Barbecue

ロース	*rōsu*	thin slices of marinated beef for roasting
上ロース	*jō-rōsu*	deluxe order of *rōsu*
カルビ	*karubi*	short rib of beef slices for roasting
ひれ/ヒレ	*hire*	slices of beef fillet meat for roasting
たん/タン	*tan*	slices of beef tongue for roasting
みの/ミノ	*mino*	slices of beef tripe for roasting
レバー	*rebā*	slices of liver for roasting
ホルモン(焼)	*horumon (yaki)*	beef giblets for roasting
はつ/ハツ	*hatsu*	beef hearts for roasting
焼やさい/焼野菜	*yaki yasai*	assorted vegetables for roasting
にんにく	*ninniku*	raw garlic for roasting

Rice Dishes

ビビンバ	bibimba	steamed rice topped with marinated bean sprouts and other vegetables
クッパ	kuppa	steamed rice in Korean-style soup
カルビクッパ	karubi kuppa	short rib of beef soup with rice
テグタン	tegutan	same as *karubi kuppa* but much spicier
ユッケジャン	yukke jan	spicy minced raw beef served over rice
おかゆ	okayu	rice gruel with vegetables and seafood

Other Dishes

ユッケ	yukke	minced beef, to be eaten raw; served with a raw egg broken over it
レバー刺	rebā sashi	raw liver *sashimi*
牛刺	gyū sashi	raw sliced beef *sashimi*
ーチゲ	-chige	spicy Korean-style stew
チャブチェ	chabuche	mixed vegetables and beef
豚足	tonsoku	steamed pig's feet
センマイ	senmai	raw tripe

Soups

カルビスープ	karubi sūpu	soup with beef-rib meat
たまごスープ/ 玉子スープ	tamago sūpu	egg soup
やさいスープ/ 野菜スープ	yasai sūpu	vegetable soup
わかめスープ	wakame sūpu	seaweed soup
テグタンスープ	tegutan sūpu	spicy *karubi* soup
もやしスープ	moyashi sūpu	bean-sprout soup

Vegetables and Pickles

キムチ	*kimuchi*	called *kim chee* in Korean: spicy pickled Chinese cabbage or other vegetables
オイキムチ	*oi-kimuchi*	spicy pickled cucumbers
ナムル	*namuru*	assorted vegetable platter
サンチュサラダ	*sanchu sarada*	Korean-style salad

Useful Phrases

Please turn (up/down) the grill.
　　Hi o (tsuyoku/yowaku) shite kudasai.
　　火を（強く/弱く）してください。

Please turn off the grill.
　　Hi o tomete kudasai.　火を止めてください。

Ramen and Chinese Food
らーめん・ラーメン・拉麺・中華

Chinese food is quite popular in Japan, although often food billed as "Chinese" has an extremely "Japanese" flavor to it. In actual fact, there are many different kinds of Chinese restaurants in Japan, but we can arbitrarily divide them into two main groups, using the criterion of authenticity. The first group includes the more authentic, regional Chinese restaurants that specialize in the cuisine of a particular area of China (such as Peking-style or Taiwanese-style). These restaurants tend to be a bit more expensive than the others, they offer a much larger number of different dishes, and they almost always advertise themselves as serving *Chūgoku ryōri* (China cuisine). At the other end of the spectrum, the second group is made up of the less expensive "Chinese-style" restaurants, which tend to concentrate on only the most popular Chinese dishes, adapted more or less to Japanese tastes. These shops usually have signs advertising *Chūka ryōri* (Chinese-style cuisine).

This second group of restaurants also contains many small shops that serve *rāmen* (from the Chinese *lao-mien*, a kind of Chinese noodle dish served in a savory soup). Ramen is the most popular Chinese dish served in Japan, and the number of ramen restaurants and stand-up counters has greatly increased in recent years. The yellow-colored ramen egg noodles are boiled and served in a hot soup—usually made from either pork or chicken bones—with a selection of different vegetables, meats and other ingredients. Many ramen restaurants are open very late, and ramen is a popular midnight snack after an evening of drinking. It's a well-known fact (among Japanese businessmen) that eating a bowl of ramen at night will help prevent a hangover the next day, and this is certainly one reason for ramen's popularity. Ramen is also a favorite of students, since it's cheap enough and substantial enough to fill the stomach without emptying the wallet.

There's a great deal of overlap between the menus of ramen shops and other inexpensive Chinese-style restaurants. Besides ramen, another popular dish in these restaurants is *yakisoba*, fried Chinese noodles served with many other ingredients. *Chāhan* is a fried rice dish, and *gyōza* and *shūmai* are two commonly served varieties of dumplings. *Gyōza* dumplings have a thick skin and are either fried or boiled, while *shūmai* have a much thinner skin and are usually steamed.

Restaurant Customs

Chinese-style restaurants can be recognized by the word *Chūka* (中華) on the sign. They are often open later than average and tend to be inexpensive. Ramen shops are even cheaper and can be recognized by the word *rāmen* (ラーメン/拉麺) on the sign.

More authentic *Chūgoku ryōri* (中国料理) and regional Chinese restaurants in Japan are more varied, and are therefore much harder to characterize in general terms. They often specify the region of their cuisine on the sign (see page 44 for examples). Taiwan and the southern regions of mainland China tend to be well represented, but restaurants of spicier regions (such as Hunan and Szechuan) are extremely rare in Japan.

Chinese restaurants in Japan share many characteristics with their counterparts throughout the world. Small groups of people are often seated together at large round tables, with lazy Susan trays in the center to make it easier to share dishes. Condiments include bottles of soy sauce, vinegar, and chili oil, and tiny sauce dishes are provided. You may be expected to eat with ornate rounded lacquered chopsticks, or beautiful ivory chopsticks, instead of the disposable square chopsticks found in most Japanese restaurants. Chinese chopsticks are longer than their Japanese counterparts, and they have smoother surfaces, making them a bit clumsy to handle even for many Japanese. Don't be surprised if they're harder to manage than you thought.

Menus are often printed in both Chinese and Japanese. The menu section in this chapter shows only the Japanese names, not the Chinese versions.

RAMEN AND CHINESE FOOD MENU

Note: Ramen shops and Chinese restaurants usually offer a wide variety of different ingredients, sauces, cooking styles, and combinations thereof. Rather than attempt to list all of the possible combinations, I've instead listed the most common ingredients and the most common types of dishes. The name of each dish is usually a combination of the main ingredients and the type of dish (i.e., "corn" + "ramen" = "ramen with corn," or "shrimp" + "chili sauce" = "shrimp in chili sauce").

Noodles and Basic Rice Dishes

TYPES OF DISHES:

−ラーメン	*-rāmen*	Chinese noodles with other ingredients in soup
−めん/麺	*-men*	Chinese noodles in soup with various condiments
−そば	*-soba*	Chinese noodles served with various toppings
−焼そば	*-yakisoba*	fried Chinese noodles
−チャーハン	*-chāhan*	fried rice
−どん/丼	*-don*	*donburi*; served over white rice in a round bowl
−ライス	*-raisu*	white rice
−スープ	*-sūpu*	soup
定食	*teishoku*	set meal with rice and soup

NOODLE AND RICE INGREDIENTS:

チャーシュー	*chāshū*	barbecued pork
チャーシューメン	*chāshū-men*	noodles in soup garnished with slices of barbecued pork
わんたん/ワンタン	*wantan*	wontons; pork-filled dumplings served in soup
みそ/味噌−	*miso-*	flavored with *miso* (soybean paste)
しお/塩−	*shio-*	with salt
バター−	*batā-*	with butter

コーン-	*kōn-*	with corn
カレー-	*karee-*	with curry sauce
五目-	*gomoku-*	"five ingredients": with assorted vegetables, seafood, and/or chicken
天津-	*tenshin-*	an egg omelette with crab and onion filling
ザーサイ-	*zāsai-*	with salty Chinese pickled turnip
タンタンメン	*tantan-men*	Chinese noodles in spicy soup
タンメン	*tan-men*	Chinese noodles in white soup
メンマ-	*menma-*	with pickled bamboo
うま煮/旨煮	*umani*	with chopped vegetables in clear, thick Chinese-style sauce
ねぎ/葱-	*negi-*	with scallions
にら/韮-	*nira-*	with leek leaves
もやし-	*moyashi-*	with bean sprouts
わかめ-	*wakame-*	with seaweed
えび/海老-	*ebi-*	with shrimp
中華丼	*Chūka-don*	chopped vegetables and bits of pork in clear, thick sauce over rice
マーボー-	*mābō-*	with tofu in a spicy sauce with ground pork
スタミナ-	*sutamina-*	with "stamina" ingredients: liver, egg, tofu, etc.
たまご/玉子-	*tamago-*	with egg
かつ丼/カツ丼	*katsu-don*	pork cutlet over rice
親子丼	*oyako-don*	chicken and egg over rice
チキン-	*chikin-*	with chicken
鳥-	*tori-*	with chicken
ソース焼そば	*sōsu yakisoba*	fried Chinese noodles with Worcestershire sauce
かた焼そば	*kata yakisoba*	deep-fried Chinese noodles topped with chopped vegetables in a clear, thick sauce

皿うどん	sara-udon	Nagasaki-style *kata yakisoba*
上海メン	*Shanhai-men*	Shanghai-style Chinese noodles
チャンポン	chanpon	Nagasaki-style ramen with assorted ingredients in soup

Appetizers

ギョーザ/餃子	gyōza	thick-skinned pork dumplings
焼ギョーザ	yaki gyōza	fried *gyōza*
揚げギョーザ	age gyōza	deep-fried *gyōza*
水ギョーザ	sui gyōza	*gyōza* served in hot soup or hot water (similar to wontons)
シューマイ/ しゅうまい	shūmai	thin-skinned pork dumplings, usually steamed
春巻	harumaki	egg rolls (lit. ''spring rolls'')
五本	go hon	five pieces
ザーサイ	zāsai	Chinese-style salt-pickled turnips
(お/御)しんこ/新香	(o)shinko	Japanese pickles
蒸し鳥	mushidori	chicken slices served with sesame oil and oyster sauce
バンバンジィ	banbanjī	strips of chicken and cucumber served in spicy ground-sesame sauce
一盛り合わせ	-moriawase	-assortment
肉まん	nikuman	pork-filled bun
焼豚	yakibuta	barbecued pork (same as *chāshū*)
鳥のから揚げ	tori no kara-age	deep-fried chicken without batter
目玉焼	medama-yaki	fried egg

Main Dishes

| 酢豚 | subuta | sweet and sour pork |
| かに玉 | kanitama | egg and crab omelette (egg fu yung) |

COOKING STYLES AND TERMS:

| 炒め | -itame | stir-fried |

一煮	-ni	stewed
一うま煮/旨煮	-umani	chopped fried vegetables in a clear, thick sauce
一辛子(ソース)煮	-karashi (sōsu) ni	in hot sauce
一クリーム煮	-kurīmu ni	in cream sauce
一煮込み	-nikomi	stewed
一煮つけ	-nitsuke	stewed (usually served in a small dish)
一角煮	-kakuni	stewed meat
一チリソース	-chiri sōsu	in chili sauce
一蒸し	-mushi	steamed
酒蒸し	-saka-mushi	steamed in saké
ごはん/御飯	-gohan	over rice
一おかゆ	-okayu	rice gruel
一揚げ	-age	deep-fried
(肉)団子	(niku) dango	meatballs, dumplings
ひき(肉)	hiki(-niku)	minced (meat)
ほそ切り/細切り	hosogiri-	shredded-
いと切り/糸切り	itogiri-	shredded-
うす切り/薄切り	usugiri-	sliced-
さいの目切り一	sainomegiri-	diced-
辛い	karai	spicy
四川風	Shisen fū	Szechuan-style
北京風	Pekin fū	Peking-style
台湾風	Taiwan fū	Taiwan-style
精進料理	shōjin ryōri	temple-style vegetarian cuisine
B 入れ A	-B- ire -A-	-A- with -B- added
C 付き	-C- tsuki	with -C- added

MAIN DISH INGREDIENTS:

Note: See "**Japanese Food Vocabulary**" section for items not listed here.

SEAFOOD:

| さかな/魚 | sakana | fish |

魚貝	gyokai	fish and shellfish
えび/海老	ebi	shrimp
しば海老/芝海老	shiba-ebi	small shrimp
小海老	ko-ebi	small shrimp
くるま海老/車海老	kuruma-ebi	prawn
大正海老	taishō-ebi	prawn
伊勢海老	Ise-ebi	Pacific langoustine
あわび/鮑	awabi	abalone
ふか/鱶(のひれ)	fuka (no hire)	shark (fins)
なまこ	namako	sea cucumber
いか	ika	squid
かに	kani	crab
かにはさみ	kani hasami	crab claws
こい/鯉	koi	carp

MEATS:

肉	niku	meat (usually pork)
豚肉	butaniku	pork
スペアリブ	supea ribu	pork spareribs
牛肉	gyūniku	beef
鳥肉	toriniku	chicken
かも/鴨	kamo	duck
ひき肉/挽肉	hikiniku	minced meat (usually pork)
レバー	rebā	liver

VEGETABLES:

やさい/野菜	yasai	vegetables
中国菜	Chūgokusai	Chinese vegetables
はくさい/白菜	hakusai	bok choy (white Chinese cabbage)
青菜	aona	Chinese greens
ピーマン	pīman	green pepper
にんにく	ninniku	garlic
にんにくの茎	ninniku no kuki	garlic shoots
にら/韮	nira	leek-like vegetable

たまねぎ/玉葱	*tamanegi*	onion
ねぎ/葱	*negi*	leek
ほうれん草	*hōrensō*	spinach
セロリ	*serori*	celery
カシューナッツ	*kashū nattsu*	cashew nuts
しいたけ/椎茸	*shiitake*	mushroom
たけのこ/竹の子	*takenoko*	bamboo shoots
なす/茄子	*nasu*	eggplant
キャベツ	*kyabetsu*	cabbage
とうふ/豆腐	*tōfu*	bean curd (tofu)
くろまめ/黒豆	*kuromame*	black (soy) beans

DESSERTS:

くだもの/果物	*kudamono*	fruit
フルーツ	*furūtsu*	fruit
ライチ	*raichi*	lychee nuts
あんまん	*anman*	bun filled with sweet red-bean paste
あん豆腐	*andōfu*	almond paste in sugar syrup with fruit

Useful Vocabulary

しょうゆ	*shōyu*	soy sauce
(お)酢	*(o)su*	vinegar
ラー油	*rāyu*	sesame oil to which red pepper has been added; also known as chili oil

Other Specialty Restaurants

In addition to the specialty restaurants covered in the preceding chapters, there are many other small eateries that specialize in one particular kind of food or another. For example, there are places that serve only sardines, or sea bream, or crabs. There are small tofu restaurants, often attached to retail tofu stores, which prepare every imaginable sort of tofu dish. There are also vegetarian restaurants, sometimes connected with Buddhist temples, which specialize in *shōjin-ryōri* (traditional Buddhist-temple vegetarian cooking). Finding these restaurants is usually a matter of hearing about them from friends or reading about them in a guidebook. For help in reading the menus, you may refer to the "**Japanese Food Vocabulary**" section at the end of the book, or you may ask the waiter or chef for recommendations (*see* "**Phrases for Ordering**," page 33). Many of these specialty restaurants serve a single set meal (or a few set meals with different prices), which makes deciding what to order much easier.

Foreign Restaurants

The larger cities in Japan, particularly Tokyo, support a healthy number of restaurants serving foreign food, ranging from French, Italian, German, and other European cuisines, to Indian, African, and Southeast Asian cooking. There are also American-style diners and fast-food restaurants. Non-European restaurants usually provide menus with English translations, while European restaurant menus tend to be in the language of the country whose cooking is represented. If you have trouble reading Italian or German or whatever, you can refer to the "**Katakana Chart**" (inside back cover) for help in reading the Japanese names of the dishes, and the "**Japanese Food Vocabulary**" section to help you figure out the ingredients used.

Japanese Desserts
デザート · 甘味(処)

Although most Japanese restaurants don't serve dessert at all, there are certain Japanese tea shops, known as *kanmi-dokoro* (sweet shops), which specialize in traditional dessert items. These shops serve Japanese sweets along with Japanese green tea, and they provide a pleasant rest stop during a day of shopping or sightseeing. There are two prevalent styles of decor, which can be termed "elegant traditional" and "rustic traditional." "Elegant traditional" decor usually features light colors, polished stone and wood, pebble gardens, and traditional Japanese artwork, while "rustic traditional" features darker colors, rough wooden beams, folk craftwork, and so forth. Many of the rustic traditional shops also serve food, such as *soba* or *kamameshi*.

The main ingredient in traditional Japanese sweets is *an*, a sweet red paste made from red adzuki beans, chestnuts, or other ingredients boiled in sugar and water. *An* is used in Japanese candies and in most of the desserts served in Japanese tea shops. Among these desserts are *anmitsu*, a cold dessert made with gelatin cubes, mandarin oranges, *an*, and a sweet dark syrup; and *kurīmu-anmitsu*, which is *anmitsu* with a scoop of vanilla ice cream on top. Another gelatin dessert is *mitsumame*, made with gelatin cubes and mixed fruits. The gelatin cubes used in these desserts are made from agar-agar, and they have a light, refreshing texture when served cold.

Other traditional sweets available at Japanese tea shops include *(o)shiruko* and *zenzai*, two warm sweet soups made from *an* and baked rice cakes (*mochi*). *Zenzai* is thicker and sweeter than *(o)shiruko*.

Tea shops also sell Japanese candies (*wagashi*), and these may be eaten in the shop or brought home or given as gifts. *Wagashi* are created for the eye as well as the palate, and they come in a multitude of shapes and colors, with different varieties for each season. Almost all of them, though, are made from the same basic ingredients—*an* paste, rice flour, wheat flour, and gelatin—so they all taste very similar, with occasional variations in texture. Since there are so many different varieties, and since many of them have flowery, poetic names, the easiest way to order *wagashi* is by pointing.

In case you can't find a Japanese tea shop, *wagashi* and other sweets are also sold in department stores. If you're in the mood for dessert, but find that Japanese sweets aren't exactly to your taste, you can often find good European-style cakes at coffee shops and cake shops (see page 145).

JAPANESE DESSERT MENU

Gelatin Desserts

みつ豆	*mitsumame*	cold agar-agar gelatin cubes, mandarin orange slices, and dark syrup
あんみつ	*anmitsu*	cold agar-agar gelatin cubes, sweet red-bean paste, dark syrup, and mandarin orange slices
クリームあんみつ	*kurīmu anmitsu*	*anmitsu* topped with vanilla ice cream
白玉あんみつ	*shiratama anmitsu*	*anmitsu* with small white rice-flour dumplings
フルーツあんみつ	*furūtsu anmitsu*	*anmitsu* with mixed fruit
マロンあんみつ	*maron anmitsu*	*anmitsu* with sweet chestnuts
栗あんみつ	*kuri anmitsu*	*anmitsu* with sweet chestnuts
小倉あんみつ	*ogura anmitsu*	*anmitsu* with whole sweet red beans
よもぎあんみつ	*yomogi anmitsu*	*anmitsu* with small green *mochi* (pounded rice) balls flavored with mugwort

Other Dessert Items

（お）しるこ	*(o)shiruko*	a warm, sweet soup made with red-bean paste and *mochi* (pounded rice) cakes
田舎（お）しるこ	*inaka (o)shiruko*	country-style *(o)shiruko* (with whole beans)
御膳（お）しるこ	*gozen (o)shiruko*	fancy *(o)shiruko* (with no whole beans)
ぜんざい	*zenzai*	a warm, thick dessert made with red-bean paste and *mochi* (pounded rice) cakes
冷しぜんざい	*hiyashi zenzai*	cold *zenzai*
いそ(べ)巻／磯(辺)巻	*iso(be)maki*	pounded rice cakes wrapped in dried *nori* seaweed, grilled, and served with soy sauce
あべ川もち	*Abekawa mochi*	*mochi* pounded rice cakes dusted with sweet soy flour
（お）雑煮	*(o)zōni*	traditional New Year's soup made with *mochi* rice cakes
よもぎ(あん)団子／だんご	*yomogi (an) dango*	small green *mochi* rice balls (with red-bean paste) flavored with mugwort
きなこ団子	*kinako dango*	*mochi* rice balls coated in sweet soybean flour
みたらし団子	*mitarashi dango*	*mochi* rice balls with sweet soy-sauce flavoring
くずきり	*kuzukiri*	cold Kansai-style pudding made from kudzu starch and served with dark syrup
ところ天	*tokoro-ten*	agar-agar gelatin noodles served with soy sauce and vinegar and topped with strips of *nori* dried seaweed
アイス(クリーム)	*aisu (kurīmu)*	ice cream (usually vanilla)
釜めし	*kamameshi*	steamed rice with seafood or other ingredients (*see* menu on page 90)

Ices

氷–	*kōri-*	shaved ice with various fruit syrups (similar to American snow cones; also called *furappe*)
氷いちご	*kōri ichigo*	shaved ice with strawberry syrup
氷あずき	*kōri azuki*	shaved ice with sweet red beans
氷ミルク	*kōri miruku*	shaved ice with sweet condensed milk
宇治氷	*Uji-gōri*	shaved ice with green tea syrup
宇治金時	*Uji kintoki*	shaved ice, red-bean paste, and green tea syrup

Coffee Shops

コーヒー・珈琲・喫茶

Japan boasts an astounding number of coffee shops. They're even more ubiquitous than the sidewalk cafes of European cities, but in Japan they serve a somewhat different social function. While European cafes are very public spaces, opening out onto the street or plaza, Japanese coffee shops are much more private, designed to serve as hideaways where one can escape from the crowds. Coffee shops are also popular places to socialize with friends or meet with business associates, since they offer more privacy and anonymity than some busy offices and cramped apartments.

Since there's such a profusion of coffee shops, competition is intense, and many shops have tried out unusual themes or peculiar gimmicks to attract customers. Coffee shop explorers can find shops where they can choose their own china, shops that are decorated like medieval castles, and shops where the chairs vibrate with the music. Other coffee shops don't go to such extremes, but still manage to attract a steady clientele through their choices of music and magazines, the quality of their food and coffee, or simply the convenience of their locations.

The quality of the coffee itself is often of secondary importance, although some shops do go to a lot of trouble over it. Whether it's good or bad, though, a cup of coffee is always fairly expensive, generally in the ¥300 to ¥500 range. What you're paying for isn't actually the coffee, but rather the privilege of sitting and relaxing in the shop. Once you've ordered a cup you can sit there as long as you like, looking at the magazines or chatting for hours on end, without being expected to order anything else.

At coffee shops which specialize in good coffee, varieties from many different coffee-growing regions of the world can be found. These coffees are identified by their region (e.g., ''Guatemala'' or ''Kenya'' coffee). Other varieties may include ''blend'' coffee, which is usually a bit stronger than usual, and "American" coffee, which most Americans would find to be a weak, insipid cup of coffee. Iced coffee is also served, although it is usually pre-sweetened. Decaffeinated coffee is almost impossible to find. Coffee shops also serve tea (regular black tea rather than Japanese-style green tea). Tea is served as either "milk tea," "lemon tea," or iced tea. At certain hours of the day, coffee and tea shops serve a "cake set," which is a cup of coffee or tea with a piece of cake at a special price.

In the morning (until about 11 AM) some coffee shops serve a "morning set" as a substitute for breakfast. A common morning set consists of a thick slice of toast with butter, a hard-boiled egg, and a cup of coffee or tea. Coffee shops sometimes serve more substantial food as well, especially at lunchtime. Western-style foods like spaghetti and rice pilaf are the general rule, along with other easily prepared foods like rice and curry or "mixed" sandwiches. A word of warning though—coffee shops are much more likely to be known for their coffee, their desserts, or their atmosphere than they are for their good food.

Coffee shops and tea shops can be found attached to most cake stores and many bakeries. They are also found in department stores, automobile showrooms, clothing boutiques, and many other places. Most shops close by 8 or 9 in the evening.

COFFEE SHOP MENU

Beverages

コーヒー/珈琲	kōhī	coffee
ホット(コーヒー)	hotto (kōhī)	hot coffee (as opposed to "iced")
アイスコーヒー	aisu kōhī	iced coffee
アメリカン	Amerikan	weak, "American-style" coffee
ブレンド	burendo	strong "blend" coffee
カフェオレ	kafe o re	café au lait

ウインナ	*uinna*	Vienna coffee, with whipped cream
カプチーノ	*kapuchīno*	cappuccino (usually strong coffee with milk and cinnamon)
モカ	*moka*	Mocha blend
紅茶	*kōcha*	black (as opposed to green) tea
ミルクティー	*miruku tī*	black tea with milk
レモンティー	*remon tī*	black tea with lemon
アイスティー	*aisu tī*	iced tea (often pre-sweetened)
ココア	*kokoa*	cocoa
オレンジジュース	*orenji jūsu*	orange-flavored drink (be careful, since this term is used both for what we call orange juice as well as orange soda)
トマトジュース	*tomato jūsu*	tomato juice or drink
ストロベリージュース	*sutoroberī jūsu*	strawberry-flavored drink
メロンジュース	*meron jūsu*	melon-flavored soda
グレープジュース	*gurēpu jūsu*	grape-flavored drink (although some places use this term for grapefruit drinks)
コーラ	*kōra*	cola
レモンスカッシュ	*remon sukasshu*	lemon-flavored drink
ヨーグルトドリンク	*yōguruto dorinku*	sweet, fruit-flavored drink made from yogurt (similar to the Indian *lassi*)
ソーダ水	*sōda-sui*	sweet, flavored soda
コーヒーフロート	*kōhī furōto*	coffee float: iced coffee with vanilla ice cream
クリームソーダ	*kurīmu sōda*	green-colored soda with vanilla ice cream

Desserts

| チョコレートケーキ | *chokorēto kēki* | chocolate cake |
| チーズケーキ | *chīzu kēki* | cheesecake (usually baked) |

レアチーズケーキ	rea chīzu kēki	gelatin-type cheesecake (unbaked)
ホットケーキ	hotto kēki	hotcakes (like pancakes about an inch thick)
プリン	purin	egg-custard pudding
コーヒーゼリー	kōhī zerī	coffee-flavored gelatin
チョコレートパフェ	chokorēto pafe	chocolate sundae with fruit
フルーツパフェ	furūtsu pafe	fruit sundae
フルーツヨーグルト	furūtsu yōguruto	yogurt with mixed fruit
フラッペ	furappe	crushed ice with fruit-flavored syrup (same as *kōri*)
氷	kōri	crushed ice with various sweet syrups (*see* **"Japanese Dessert Menu,"** page 142)

Sandwiches

サンド(イッチ)	sando(itchi)	sandwich
エッグ	eggu	egg
たまご/玉子	tamago	egg
ハム	hamu	ham
ツナ	tsuna	tuna salad
やさい/野菜	yasai	vegetables (usually sliced cucumber and tomato with mayonnaise)
ミックス	mikkusu	mixed assortment of the above
コンビネーション	konbinēshon	combination of the above
トースト	tōsuto	thickly sliced toast
ピザトースト	piza tōsuto	pizza toast
ツナトースト	tsuna tōsuto	tuna salad on toast
チーズトースト	chīzu tōsuto	toast with melted cheese
モーニングセット	mōningu setto	"morning set": coffee, toast, and sometimes a hard-boiled egg
ピザ	piza	miniature pizza, served with Tabasco sauce

Other Food Items

スパゲッティ	*supagetti*	spaghetti
ボロネーズ	*boronēzu*	meat sauce (Bolonaise)
ミートソース	*mīto sōsu*	meat sauce
カルボナーラ	*karubonāra*	cream sauce with bacon and mushrooms
ナポリタン	*naporitan*	tomato sauce with vegetables
グラタン	*guratan*	something baked au gratin
えびグラタン/ 海老グラタン	*ebi guratan*	baked macaroni au gratin with shrimp
シーフードグラタン	*shīfūdo guratan*	seafood au gratin
シーフードドリア	*shīfūdo doria*	baked rice with cheese and seafood
えびピラフ/ 海老ピラフ	*ebi pirafu*	shrimp pilaf
チキンピラフ	*chikin pirafu*	chicken pilaf
ドライカレー	*dorai karē*	curried pilaf
カレーライス	*karē raisu*	white rice with curry sauce (usually beef if not otherwise specified)
しょうが焼/ 生姜焼	*shōgayaki*	pork sautéed with ginger and onions
ハンバーグ （ステーキ）	*hanbāgu (sutēki)*	ground beef patty with gravy and rice
サラダ	*sarada*	green salad

Boxed Lunches and Food Delivery

べんとう・弁当・出前

Bentō Lunches and Department Stores

Bentō lunches are convenient boxed meals that are very popular for office or picnic lunches. Bentō boxes include a compartment filled with rice, and several other compartments containing a variety of prepared foods, usually those which keep well and which taste good when eaten cold. Home-prepared bentō often come in special red lacquerware boxes, although plastic boxes are becoming more popular. Train stations (*eki*) also sell bentō lunches, called *eki-ben*, and certain train stations throughout Japan have their own special varieties of bentō that they've become famous for. There are also specialty bentō stores that sell both hot and cold boxed lunches. At bentō stores the *makunouchi bentō* is the "special of the house"; it's changed daily and it may include items like smoked fish; steamed, salted vegetables; fish cakes; pickles; and, of course, rice. Restaurants and food-delivery services also serve bentō meals; these include a variety of foods, and they are also served in compartmentalized plastic boxes.

Another place to buy boxed lunches is in department stores. Many major department stores in Japan have a "food floor" in the basement, where they sell a dazzling variety of fresh foods, prepared dishes, and imported delicacies. There are rows and rows of small stands where you can buy take-home portions of tempura, *yakitori,* and everything else imaginable. The fresh-food areas are crowded with fish sellers and vegetable vendors loudly hawking their wares, while the imported-food sections strive for a quieter and more opulent feeling. Food floors of department stores present an intriguing mixture of the fancy shopping district and the raucous street market, and they're well worth a visit.

Bentō lunches sold in train stations and on food floors are usually displayed in sample form, so you can just point to what you want. You may also refer to the "**Nihon-ryōri**" chapter and the "**Japanese Food Vocabulary**" lists for help in reading their names.

Getting Food Delivered

If you live in an apartment or house in Japan, from time to time you'll probably find delivery menus from local restaurants in your mailbox. You may also ask for them at local restaurants. (Places that deliver can be identified by the delivery bikes parked outside.) Ask if they deliver as far as your home, and make sure to find out when their delivery hours are (they should be listed on the menu). Restaurants serving sushi, *soba*, and Chinese food are the most likely to deliver, although recently pizzerias have also begun to spring up. Sometimes there's a minimum order for delivery, so if you plan to order just one meal, you should first ask if it's okay. When you've finished eating, rinse out the trays and dishes you've used (you don't have to be too thorough, since they'll be washed again) and leave them outside your door, where they'll be picked up. Delivery persons in Japan don't expect to be tipped.

Useful phrases for food delivery can be found below, after the sample bentō menu.

BENTŌ MENU

べんとう/弁当	*bentō*	boxed lunch
幕の内	*makunouchi*	special of the day (or special of the shop)
日替わり	*higawari*	special of the day
のり/海苔	*nori*	plain rice topped with strips of dried seaweed (usually very inexpensive)
さけ(しゃけ)/鮭	*sake (or shake)*	plain rice with a small piece of salmon (very inexpensive)
カレーライス	*karē raisu*	rice with curry sauce

親子丼	*oyako don*	chicken and egg over rice
とんかつ/トンカツ	*tonkatsu*	deep-fried pork cutlet
かつ重/カツ重	*katsu jū*	pork cutlet on rice
天重	*ten jū*	tempura-fried prawn on rice
海老フライ	*ebi furai*	fried shrimp
メンチかつ	*menchi katsu*	deep-fried meat patty
ミックスフライ	*mikkusu furai*	fried beef patty, croquettes, and/or shrimp
ハンバーグ	*hanbāgu*	hamburg patty
焼肉	*yakiniku*	marinated slices of grilled meat
から揚げ/唐揚げ	*kara-age*	deep-fried chicken
ステーキ	*sutēki*	minute steak
うなぎ/鰻	*unagi*	grilled eel

RICE AND SUSHI:

ライス	*raisu*	rice
おにぎり	*onigiri*	rice balls wrapped in dried seaweed
のり巻/海苔巻	*nori-maki*	rice and other ingredients rolled in dried seaweed
太巻	*futo-maki*	rice, vegetables, cooked egg, and other ingredients in a fat roll of dried seaweed
いなり鮨/稲荷鮨	*inari-zushi*	rice wrapped in a bag of fried tofu
押し鮨	*oshi-zushi*	Osaka-style sushi; cooked fish pressed over vinegared rice
みそ汁/味噌汁	*miso shiru*	*miso* (soybean paste) soup

FOOD DELIVERY VOCABULARY

出前	*demae*	delivery service

営業時間	eigyō jikan	hours (when the store is open)
（午前11時）より	(gozen jū-ichi ji) yori	from 11 AM
（午後9時）まで	(gogo ku ji) made	until 9 PM
定休日	teikyūbi	weekly holiday (day off)
日（曜日）	nichi(yōbi)	Sunday
月（曜日）	getsu(yōbi)	Monday
火（曜日）	ka(yōbi)	Tuesday
水（曜日）	sui(yōbi)	Wednesday
木（曜日）	moku(yōbi)	Thursday
金（曜日）	kin(yōbi)	Friday
土（曜日）	do(yōbi)	Saturday
祭日	saijitsu	national holidays
日曜祭日も営業	nichiyō saijitsu mo eigyō	open Sundays and holidays
年中無休	nenjū mukyū	open every day of the year
電話（番号）	denwa (bangō)	telephone (number)

Useful Phrases

Do you deliver as far as XX?　*XX made demae dekimasu ka?*
XX まで出前できますか？

Do you have a delivery menu?
Demae-yō no menyū wa arimasu ka?
出前用のメニューはありますか？

I'd like to order something to be delivered.
Demae onegai shimasu.　出前お願いします。

We've stopped delivering.
Demae wa mō owarimashita.　出前はもう終わりました。

What's your address?
Jūsho oshiete kudasai.　住所教えてください。

What's your name and telephone number?
O-namae to denwa bango o itadakemasu ka?
お名前と電話番号をいただけますか？

Drinking in Japan
さけ・サケ・酒

Where to Drink

The adventurous explorer can find an extraordinary variety of drinking places in Japan. These range from seedy nighttime stalls on busy sidewalks to luxurious hostess bars in the heart of Tokyo's Ginza district. With all this variety, it shouldn't be difficult to find a perfect watering hole for any occasion or mood.

The most economical places to drink are *izakaya* (pubs) and certain pub-like restaurants, such as *yakitori-ya*, *kushiage-ya*, and *oden-ya*. *Izakaya* (also called *nomi-ya*) strive for a friendly, down-to-earth atmosphere, and they feature inexpensive food as well as drinks. Alcoholic beverages are usually limited to beer, *shōchū*, and sometimes whiskey. **Beer gardens** are similar to *izakaya*, but are located on the roofs of department stores and are open only in the summertime.

Regular **bars** tend to be much smaller than their Western counterparts, and large buildings will often contain dozens of tiny bars, each with room for only five or ten people. These small places have a private, intimate atmosphere, and walking into them is like walking into someone's living room. By the same token, walking in uninvited can be a bit uncomfortable, so it's usually best to go with someone who's a regular patron.

There are of course larger bars that are more friendly to strangers. Both large and small bars, though, develop loyal patrons who become regulars. To further encourage this loyalty, bars in Japan employ what they call a "keep bottle" system: This means that you can buy a bottle of liquor (usually whiskey) and have the bartender keep it for you between visits. Just about every bar in Japan has shelves or cabinets filled with keep bottles, each with the name of the owner written in waterproof marker on the label. Very traditional bars will also have keep bottles of saké, while very modern ones will let you keep bottles of bourbon or other liquors. Because of space limitations, keep bottles are only kept for three to six months or so after your last visit.

Discotheques are also smaller than their Western counterparts, although they're larger than regular bars. Many of them cater to a young crowd, and most serve food. Some discotheques are very economical: Often the price of admission will include free food and drink tickets, or even an open bar and an all-you-can-eat buffet. Discotheques and larger bars serve mixed drinks as well as beer and whiskey.

Hostess bars are bars that employ "hostesses" to light cigarettes, stir drinks, and make conversation with the customers. Although most hostess bars are used for legitimate business entertaining, they all tend to charge high prices (sometimes extremely high).

Karaoke bars are bars that provide microphones and background music and encourage their customers to take turns singing popular songs. If your idea of a fun evening is listening to strangers in various states of drunkenness singing badly in a language you don't understand, then a *karaoke* bar is the best place to go. They're enormously popular, and can be found in any entertainment district (just listen for the music).

Although *izakaya* are referred to in this book as pubs, there is also a Japanese word **pabu** (pronounced "pub"), which refers to a different type of bar. *Pabu* bars are usually small places with Western-style decor, and they often double as coffee shops during the day. Another confusing Japanese term is **sunakku** (pronounced "snack"). "Snack" bars serve tiny dishes of food with their drinks, and this somehow allows them to stay open later and charge more money than regular bars. "Snack" bars are often open well past the last train of the night (which is usually around midnight or 1 AM). Both "pub" and "snack" bars serve whiskey and beer, and they often feature *karaoke* singing.

Precautions When Selecting a Bar

In Japanese business life, drinking and "business entertainment" play an important role in cementing relations between individuals who do business together. One way to show an important client how important he is is to spend a lot of money entertaining him. This practice has created a whole class of "expense-account bars." Some of these bars will charge hundreds or even thousands of dollars for an evening's drinks, all for the purpose of impressing a client with how much expense-account money he rates. Not all expensive and super-expensive bars look the part, either; many of them are quite discreet, or even ordinary-looking.

If you're looking for a place to drink without an expense account, the best idea is to go somewhere that's recommended by friends. If you're going to a bar you don't know, it's always a good idea to check the prices first, and of course avoid hostess bars and places with touts outside, which are always overpriced. If you're looking for an economical evening out and you don't mind a very informal atmosphere, *izakaya* can be interesting and fun, and they're always inexpensive.

What People Drink

Beer is by far the most popular alcoholic beverage in Japan, and it's served at almost every restaurant and bar. It's also available from sidewalk vending machines, at kiosks in train stations, and in liquor stores. At restaurants and pubs it's usually available in large bottles and sometimes on draft, while in cafe bars and coffee shops it often comes in smaller cans.

Saké, or rice wine, is also popular at certain restaurants and pubs, particularly those serving traditional Japanese food. Saké can be served either hot or cold, but hot saké is more popular in wintertime. There are thousands of different brands of saké from all over Japan, but most restaurants have chosen a "house" brand that they serve.

Whiskey is the most popular hard liquor, and it's traditionally served as *mizuwari* (with water and ice). **Shōchū** is a distilled grain alcohol that recently underwent a surge in popularity, although its sales are now leveling off. Good *shōchū* is similar to vodka, although a bit less smooth, while cheap *shōchū* is closer to kerosene in taste and effect. It's usually served as a *chūhai* (a shō-*chū* high*ball*), which is *shōchū* mixed with a sweet soda or fruit drink.

Wine is available at some restaurants, but usually only those serving Western-style cuisine or *teppanyaki*. **Mixed drinks** are even harder to find, except at medium-to-large-sized bars (including hotel bars).

Liquor stores sell beer, saké, wine, and various liquors, and "combination stores" sell both food and liquor. Regular food stores, unless they have a special license, aren't allowed to sell any alcoholic beverages, even beer. Liquor stores often have sidewalk vending machines that dispense beer and whiskey. These vending machines are supposed to stop selling at 11 PM, although the stores themselves may stay open later. Liquor stores in smaller neighborhoods sometimes sell liquor by the drink, and often they get a small crowd of stand-up drinkers in the early evening.

Drinking Customs

Saké, which is the most traditional drink, has many customs associated with it, and these customs have been extended to apply to other drinks as well. The first rule is that one doesn't pour for oneself (at least not at the beginning); first the host fills the cup (or glass) of the guest, then vice versa. The person whose cup is being poured should raise his cup a little bit off the table (this also applies to beer and whiskey). Whether you're host or guest, it's very important to pay attention to whether the other person's glass is empty (since he might think it rude to refill it himself). When you're drinking beer, it's more acceptable to pour for yourself, but only after you've filled everyone else's glass first. The usual toast is "*Kampai*," which literally means "Empty the glass" or "Bottoms up!"

In restaurants, drinks are generally accompanied by hors d'oeuvres rather than the main course. This is particularly true with saké, which is never served at the same time as rice. Many bars and pubs bring a tiny dish of food (called an *otōshi*, or *otsumami*) with your first drink. This is added to your final bill, as is the "ice charge" if you're drinking from your keep bottle. These charges tend to make bar hopping more expensive than simply settling down in one bar for the evening.

Drinking at lunchtime is fairly rare, but many people make up for it in the evening. Public drunkenness is much more tolerated than it is in most Western countries; according to some sociological experts it serves as a "safety valve" in a society with an otherwise rigid social structure. The official drinking age is twenty, but this law is widely ignored. One exception to this lenient attitude is when it comes to driving: The laws are very strict, and anything over one drink is likely to trigger the electronic alcohol testers used by the police during random traffic checks.

Hangovers

According to the results of an informal survey, the worst hangovers by far are produced by *shōchū*, particularly in its mixed-drink "*chūhai*" form. Saké isn't quite as bad, but it's fairly smooth and easy to drink too much of, especially if it's heated. Eating a bowl of *rāmen* noodles after drinking is said to reduce the chances of a hangover. There's also a major industry devoted to selling "sports drinks" and "isotonic beverages," which are quite popular as hangover remedies.

COCKTAIL AND BEVERAGE MENU

Drinks in Restaurants

ビール	*bīru*	beer
生ビール	*nama bīru*	draft beer
黒生ビール	*kuro nama bīru*	dark draft beer
大きい/大/大	*ōkii/ō/dai*	large
普通/中	*futsū/chū*	(regular) medium
小さい/小/小	*chiisai/ko/shō*	small
日本酒	*Nihon-shu*	Japanese saké
(お/御)さけ/酒	*(o)saké*	Japanese saké
ウイスキー	*uisukī*	whiskey
水割り	*mizuwari*	whiskey and water
ボトル	*botoru*	bottle (usually a "keep" bottle of whiskey)
焼酎	*shōchū*	Japanese grain liquor
酎ハイ	*chūhai*	*shōchū* highball
サワー	*sawā*	usually a *shōchū* "sour"
レモンサワー	*remon sawā*	lemon-flavored *shōchū* sour
ライムサワー	*raimu sawā*	lime sour

ウメ(梅)サワー	*ume sawā*	plum-flavored sour
ウーロンサワー	*ūron sawā*	*shōchū* and oolong tea
ワイン	*wain*	wine
赤ワイン	*aka wain*	red wine
白ワイン	*shiro wain*	white wine
グラスワイン	*gurasu wain*	a glass of wine
ジュース	*jūsu*	fruit-flavored drink (also a generic term for soft drinks, sodas, etc.)
オレンジ	*orenji*	orange drink
コーラ	*kōra*	cola

Bar Drinks and Phrases for Ordering

Note: Names of cocktails are usually written in *katakana*, so you may be able to read the names of cocktails not found below by referring to the "**Katakana Chart**" on the inside back cover.

ウォッカ	*uokka*	vodka
ジン	*jin*	gin
バーボン	*bābon*	bourbon
スコッチ	*sukotchi*	Scotch whisky
ラム	*ramu*	rum (note, however, that on restaurant menus, *ramu* means lamb)
ジントニック	*jin tonikku/ jin-ton*	gin and tonic
マティーニ	*matīni*	martini (often this will contain no gin, just vermouth on the rocks, so don't be surprised if you're asked "Sweet or dry?")
スクリュードライバー	*sukuryūdoraibā*	screwdriver
ソーダ割り	*sōdawari*	Scotch and soda
ペリエ	*Perie*	Perrier mineral water
炭酸	*tansan*	club soda
ジンジャエール	*jinja ēru*	ginger ale
トニックウォーター	*tonikku uōtā*	tonic water

One (two) bottles of beer, please.
Bīru o ippon (nihon) kudasai.
ビールを一本(二本)ください。

Medium-sized (draft) beer, please.
Chū (nama) bīru o kudasai. 中(生)ビールをください。

Large-sized (draft) beer, please.
Dai (nama) bīru o kudasai. 大(生)ビールをください。

Japanese Food Vocabulary and Glossary

Note: In many cases the "Japanese-English" versions of English terms (e.g., *pīchi* for peach) have been omitted when there is a corresponding Japanese word. The numbers listed after some of the entries refer to page numbers in the text.

A

Abekawa-mochi (あべ川餅)   *kinako*-covered pounded rice cakes served as a dessert

abura (油)   oil

abura-age (油揚げ)   fried slices of tofu

aemono (和え物)   foods dressed with vinegar or sauces

agari (あがり)   green tea served with sushi [53]

-age (揚げ)   fried

agedashi-dōfu (揚げ出し豆腐)   fried tofu (*atsu-age*) topped with condiments and served in a warm soy-based broth

age-dōfu (揚げ豆腐)   fried tofu served with grated *daikon* and soy sauce

ahiru (あひる)   (domesticated) duck

aigamo (合鴨)   duck (a cross between a domesticated and a wild duck)

ainame (あいなめ)   rock trout

aisu-kōhī (アイスコーヒー)   iced coffee

aisu-kurīmu (アイスクリーム)   ice cream

aisu-tī (アイスティー)   iced tea

aji (味)   flavor, taste

aji (鯵)   horse mackerel

aka chōchin (赤ちょうちん)   pub-style restaurant with red lanterns outside [107]

akadashi (赤だし)   soup made from dark brown *miso*

akagai (赤貝)   ark shell

amadai (甘鯛)   red tilefish

ama-ebi (甘海老)   raw shrimp

ama-guri (甘栗)   roast chestnuts

ama(i) (甘い)   sweet

amiyaki (網焼)   cooked over a wire grill

an (あん)   sweet jam made from adzuki beans; also called *anko* (あんこ) [141]

anago (穴子)   conger eel

ankō (鮟鱇)   angler fish

ankō nabe (鮟鱇鍋)   stew made from *ankō*

anmitsu (あんみつ)   dessert made with agar-agar cubes, *an*, syrup, and fruit [141]

anzu (杏)   apricot

aoyagi (青柳)   round clam

arai (あらい)   raw fish, thinly sliced (thinner than *sashimi*), artfully arranged, and served on ice

ara-ni (あら煮)   stewed fish

arare (あられ)   pellet-shaped *senbei* crackers

asa gohan (朝御飯)   breakfast

asari (あさり)   short-necked clam

asatsuki (あさつき)   chives

asupara (アスパラ)   asparagus

atsu-age (厚揚)   fried tofu blocks

awabi (鮑)   abalone

ayu (鮎)   sweetfish

azuki (小豆)   adzuki beans

B

banana (バナナ)   banana

bancha (番茶)   ordinary-grade green tea

baniku (馬肉)   horsemeat

banira (バニラ)   vanilla

basashi (馬刺)   raw horsemeat served *sashimi*-style

batā (バター)   butter

battera-zushi (バッテラ寿司)   Osaka-style molded mackerel sushi

bēkon (ベーコン)   bacon

bentō (弁当)   boxed lunch [150]

bīfu (ビーフ)   beef

bīfun (ビーフン)   thin, Chinese-style rice noodles

bīru (ビール)   beer [156]

biwa (びわ)   loquat; medlar fruit

botan-nabe (牡丹鍋)   a stew made with boar meat [93]

budō (葡萄)   grapes

buri (鰤)   yellowtail (fish)

burokkorī (ブロッコリー)   broccoli

burūberī (ブルーベリー)   blueberry

butaniku (豚肉)   pork

C

(o)cha ([お]茶)   green tea

chāhan (チャーハン)   fried rice with various ingredients

chai (チャイ)   Indian-style milk tea, often spiced with ginger and cardamom *chanko-nabe* (ちゃんこ鍋)　seafood and vegetable stew often eaten by sumo wrestlers [92]

chanpon (チャンポン)　Nagasaki-style *rāmen* in soup

chawan (茶碗)　rice bowl

chawan mushi (茶碗蒸し)　a savory custard made with eggs, diced vegetables, and chicken

chazuke (茶漬)　rice flavored with various toppings, over which green tea has been poured

chikin (チキン)　chicken

chikuwa (竹輪)　hollow, tube-shaped fish cake [99]

chirashi-zushi (ちらし寿司)　assorted raw fish over a bed of rice [54]

chiri-nabe (ちり鍋)　quick-cooked stew made with cod or other fish

chīzu (チーズ)　cheese

chokorēto (チョコレート)　chocolate

chōmi ryō (調味料)　seasonings, flavorings

chūhai (酎ハイ)　a *shōchū* cocktail [156]

chūka-don (中華丼)　bits of pork and vegetables in a clear sauce over rice

chūkafū (中華風)　Chinese-style [132]

chūmon (suru) (注文[する])　(to) order

chū toro (中とろ)　somewhat fatty, pink tuna

D

daidai (橙)　a bitter orange

daifuku (大福)　a Japanese rice cake filled with sweet bean jam

daikon (大根)　Japanese radish

daizu (大豆)　soybeans

dango (団子)　dumpling

dashi (だし)　fish and kelp-flavored stock

date-maki (伊達巻)　a kind of flat, sweet omelette made from ground fish eggs, rolled and served in slices

demae (出前)　delivery service [151]

denbu (でんぶ)　pink, crumbled fish paste

dengaku (田楽)　*konnyaku* or tofu broiled with sweetened *miso*

dezāto (デザート)　dessert

dojō (どじょう/どぜう)　loach (eel-like fish) [62]

-don(buri) (―丼)　meat or other ingredients served over a bowl of rice

dote-nabe (土手鍋)　a stew made with oysters and *miso*

E

ebi (海老)　shrimp

edamame (枝豆)　green soybeans

ei(hire) (えい[ひれ])　(fillet of) ray

ekiben (駅弁)   *bentō*-style boxed lunches sold specially in train stations
endō(mame) (えんどう[豆])   peas
enoki(dake) (えのき[茸])   a thin, white mushroom used in stews

F

fōku (フォーク)   fork
fu (麩)   a fluffy cake of wheat gluten
fugu (河豚)   blowfish; globefish [64]
fuka (鱶)   shark
fuki (蕗)   coltsfoot (vegetable)
fukujin-zuke (福神漬)   the red pickles customarily served with curry dishes in non-Indian restaurants in Japan
furūtsu (フルーツ)   fruit
futsukayoi (二日酔い)   hangover [158]

G

Note: The initial syllable "go" is often an honorific prefix in Japanese (as in *gohan*). If you don't find a word beginning with "go" in the section below, check under the second syllable of the word.

ganmodoki (がんもどき)   fried tofu patties with bits of vegetables
gari (がり)   sliced ginger served in sushi restaurants
gatsu (がつ)   intestines ("guts")
genmai (玄米)   unpolished (brown) rice
geppei (月餅)   "moon cake": Chinese pastry stuffed with fruit and nuts
geso (下足)   squid tentacles
ginnan (銀杏)   ginkgo nuts
ginpō (ぎんぽう)   gunnel (fish)
gobō (ごぼう)   burdock root
Gochisō sama. (ごちそうさま。)   "Thanks for the great meal."
gohan (御飯)   literally, rice; but often used to mean meal
goma (胡麻)   sesame seeds
goma-shio (胡麻塩)   sesame seeds mixed with salt
gomoku (五目)   an assortment of many ingredients (added to rice or noodles)
guratan (グラタン)   au gratin
gurēpufurūtsu (グレープフルーツ)   grapefruit
gyokai (魚貝)   fish and shellfish
gyokuro (玉露)   deluxe grade of green tea
gyōza (餃子)   Chinese-style pork dumplings [133]
gyūniku (牛肉)   beef
gyūnyū (牛乳)   milk

H

hachimitsu (はちみつ)   honey

hakumai (白米)   polished rice

hakusai (白菜)   bok choy (Chinese cabbage)

hamachi (はまち)   young yellowtail (fish)

hamaguri (蛤)   clam

hamu (ハム)   ham

hanbāgā (ハンバーガー)   hamburger

hanbāgu (ハンバーグ)   hamburger steak

hanpen (半ぺん)   a soft white fish cake made with yam

harusame (春雨)   "spring rain": extremely thin, translucent noodles made from various starches

hasami (はさみ)   "scissors"; seafood: crab or shellfish claws; *yakitori*: alternating pieces of chicken and leek on a skewer

hashi (箸)   chopsticks [30, 133]

hasu (蓮)   lotus (root)

hatsu (はつ)   heart

hayashi raisu (ハヤシライス)   sliced beef and onion in gravy, served over rice

haze (はぜ)   goby (fish)

hijiki (ひじき)   brown algae used in cooking

hikiniku (挽肉)   ground meat

himono (干物)   dried fish or shellfish

hirame (平目)   flounder

hire (ヒレ[肉])   fillet

hire (鰭)   fin

hire-zake (鰭酒)   hot saké flavored with roasted *fugu* fins

hiru-gohan (昼御飯)   lunch

(o)hitashi ([お]ひたし)   boiled greens served with soy sauce and dried bonito flakes

(o)hiya ([お]冷)   cold water; cold (saké)

hiyamugi (冷麦)   thin wheat noodles served cold

hiyashi (冷し)   cold

hiyashi-bachi (冷し鉢)   served in a bowl with ice and cold water

hiya yakko (冷奴)   blocks of tofu served cold

hōjicha (ほうじ茶)   roasted green tea

hokke (ほっけ)   Atka mackerel

hone (骨)   bone

hōrensō (ほうれん草)   spinach

hōroku-yaki (ほうろく焼)   baked with salt in a covered earthenware dish

hoshi (干)   dried

hoshi-budō (乾葡萄)   raisins

hotategai (帆立貝)   scallop

hoya (ほや)　　sea squirt

hyaku-pāsento (jūsu) (100%[ジュース])　　100% (juice)

I

ichigo (苺)　　strawberry

ichijiku (いちじく)　　fig

ichimi (一味)　　a powdered red pepper

iidako (いい蛸)　　a small octopus

ika (いか)　　squid; also used to mean cuttlefish

ikura (いくら)　　salmon roe

imo (芋)　　generic term for any kind of potato

inada (いなだ)　　very young yellowtail (fish)

inari-zushi (稲荷寿司)　　sushi rice wrapped in fried tofu [54]

ingen(mame) (隠元[豆])　　string beans

inoshishi (猪)　　wild boar

inshokuzei (飲食税)　　restaurant tax [32]

ippin ryōri (一品料理)　　a la carte items

-iri (-入り)　　stuffed with; including

isaki (いさき)　　grunt (fish)

ise-ebi (伊勢海老)　　Pacific spiny lobster (similar to a langouste)

ishikari-nabe (石狩鍋)　　Hokkaido-style salmon stew

isobe-maki (磯辺巻)　　grilled *mochi* wrapped in seaweed

itamae (板前)　　chef in a *ryōtei* or other restaurant; said especially of those who prepare sushi

-itame (-炒め)　　stir-fried

itawasa (板わさ)　　*kamaboko* fish-cake slices served with green horseradish

iwashi (鰯)　　sardine

izakaya (居酒屋)　　pub-style restaurant [107,154]

J

jagaimo (じゃがいも)　　common white potato

jamu (ジャム)　　jam

jin (ジン)　　gin

-jū (-重)　　meat or other ingredients served over rice in a rectangular box

jūsu (ジュース)　　fruit-flavored drink

K

kabayaki (蒲焼)　　grilled eel [61]

kabocha (南瓜)　　pumpkin

kabu (かぶ)　　a small white turnip

kai (貝)　　literally, shellfish; a generic term for shellfish

kaibashira (貝柱)　　valve muscle of a mollusk (esp. scallop)

kaiseki ryōri (会席料理)   traditional, expensive Kyoto-style cuisine originally associated with the tea ceremony [28, 120]

kaisō (海草)   seaweed

kaiware (かいわれ)   *daikon* shoots, used as a garnish

kake soba (掛け蕎麦)   *soba* noodles served with a hot broth [72]

kaki (柿)   persimmon

kaki (かき)   oyster

kakiage (かき揚げ)   diced shrimp fried tempura-style

kamaboko (蒲鉾)   a white fish cake used in stews and soups

kamameshi (釜飯)   rice steamed with seafood and vegetables [89]

kamasu (かます)   barracuda

kamo (鴨)   (wild) duck

kani (かに)   crab

kani-miso (かにみそ)   crab guts

kanmi-dokoro (甘味処)   a traditional Japanese sweet shop [141]

kanpyō (かんぴょう)   dried gourd shavings

kanten (寒天)   agar-agar

kanzume (缶詰)   canned (food)

kappa-maki (かっぱ巻)   rolled cucumber sushi

kappō (割烹)   a restaurant serving a variety of Japanese dishes [120]

kara-age (唐揚げ)   deep-fried without batter

karai (辛い)   spicy; also, sometimes, salty

kara-senbei (からせんべい)   spicy Japanese crackers

karashi (辛子)   Japanese mustard

karē (カレー)   curry; curried dish served with rice

karei (かれい)   flounder

(o)karibayaki ([御]狩場焼)   "hunter's grill": skewered game birds and vegetables

karifurawā (カリフラワー)   cauliflower

karubi (カルビ)   Korean term for beef rib meat [128]

(o)kashi ([お]菓子)   generic term for sweets

katsu-don (カツ丼)   pork cutlet served over rice (in a bowl)

katsuo (鰹)   bonito

katsuo-bushi (鰹ぶし)   dried bonito flakes [102]

kawa-ebi (川海老)   freshwater shrimp

kazunoko (数の子)   herring roe

kechappu (ケチャップ)   catsup (ketchup)

keishoku (軽食)   a light meal

kēki (ケーキ)   cake

kiichigo (木苺)   raspberry

kiji-jū (きじ重)   grilled chicken slices (lit. "pheasant") over rice

kikuna (菊菜)   edible chrysanthemum

kikurage (きくらげ)　wood ear (tree fungus)

kimi (黄身)　egg yolk

kimosui (肝吸い)　a clear soup made with eel livers [62]

kimo(yaki) (肝[焼])　(grilled) liver

kimuchi (キムチ)　*kim chee*; spicy Korean-style pickled bok choy [128]

kinako (きな粉)　soybean flour

kinoko (きのこ)　generic term for mushrooms

kinome (木の芽)　prickly-ash leaves, used as a garnish

kinpira (きんぴら)　julienned carrots and burdock root stewed in soy sauces and spices

kishimen (きしめん)　flat white wheat noodles

kissaten (喫茶店)　coffee shop [145]

kisu (きす)　sillago (fish)

kōcha (紅茶)　black tea

ko-ebi (小海老)　small shrimp

kohada (こはだ)　gizzard shad (fish)

kōhī (珈琲)　coffee [145]

ko-hitsuji (子羊)　lamb

koi (鯉)　carp

kokoa (ココア)　cocoa

kokonattsu (ココナッツ)　coconut

kokumotsu (穀物)　a generic term for any type of grain

(o)kome ([お]米)　uncooked rice

komugiko (小麦粉)　wheat flour

kōn (コーン)　corn

konbīfu (コンビーフ)　corned beef

konbu (昆布)　kelp

konnyaku (こんにゃく)　blocks of translucent, gelatinous devil's-tongue starch

konyakku (コニャック)　cognac

kōra (コーラ)　cola

kōra (甲羅)　shell; shellfish cooked in its shell

kōri (氷)　ice

korokke (コロッケ)　croquette [79]

kōshinryō (香辛料)　herbs and spices

koshō (こしょう)　black pepper

kōsu (コース)　full-course meal [31]

ko-ushi(niku) (子牛[肉])　veal

kudamono (果物)　fruit

kujira (鯨)　whale

kukkī (クッキー)　cookie

kurēpu (クレープ)　crepe

kuri (栗)   chestnut

kurīmu (クリーム)   cream

kuruma-ebi (車海老)   a type of prawn

kurumi (くるみ)   walnut

kushi-age (串揚)   deep-fried seafood on skewers [81]

kushi-yaki (串焼)   any skewered food, including *kushi-age* and *yakitori*

kuwai (くわい)   water chestnut

kuzu (くず)   the kudzu plant or its cornflour-like starch

kyabetsu (キャベツ)   cabbage

kyūri (きゅうり)   cucumber

M

mābō-dōfu (マーボー豆腐)   tofu cubes in a spicy meat sauce

māgarin (マーガリン)   margarine

maguro (鮪)   tuna

-maki (－巻)   rolled

maku-no-uchi (*bentō*) (幕の内[弁当])   "special of the house" (now used almost exclusively for *bentō* lunches; the name literally means "between the acts," since this type of boxed lunch originally became popular among those spending the day watching Kabuki) [150]

mame (豆)   a generic term for any type of bean

mangō (マンゴー)   mango

manjū (饅頭)   a steamed bun filled with sweet red-bean paste or some other filling, like ground meat

maron (マロン)   chestnut

-maru-yaki (－丸焼)   a whole fish (or bird) served grilled

masu (鱒)   trout

masukatto (マスカット)   muscat grapes

masutādo (マスタード)   Western-style mustard; also called *yō-garashi*

matcha (抹茶)   powdered green tea

maton (マトン)   mutton

matsutake (松茸)   "pine mushroom": an expensive toadstool-shaped mushroom prized for its exceptional aroma

mayonēzu (マヨネーズ)   mayonnaise

mazui (まずい)   bad(-tasting)

megochi (めごち)   flathead (fish)

mekajiki (めかじき)   swordfish

mekyabetsu (芽キャベツ)   Brussels sprouts

menrui (麺類)   generic term for noodles

mentaiko (明太子)   cod roe mixed with salt and/or red pepper

menyū (メニュー)   menu

meron (メロン)   melon

meshi (飯)　cooked rice; it can also mean "meal"

mikan (みかん)　mandarin orange; tangerine

mirin (みりん)　sweetened cooking saké

mirugai (みる貝)　surf clam

miruku (ミルク)　milk; but the word is often used to mean the cream one uses in coffee (what we call milk is called *gyūnyū*)

miso (味噌)　fermented soybean paste used as a flavoring

miso-shiru (味噌汁)　soup flavored with *miso*

mitsuba (三つ葉)　trefoil leaf used as a garnish in clear soups

mitsumame (みつ豆)　a dessert made with agar-agar cubes, syrup, and fruit [141]

mizu (水)　water

mizutaki (水炊き)　chicken and vegetable *nabe*-style stew

mizuwari (水割り)　whiskey and water [156]

mochi (餅)　pounded rice cakes made of glutinous rice

mochigome (餅米)　glutinous rice

mochikaeri (持ち帰り)　takeout; these days, also called *tēkauto*

momo (桃)　peach

momo (もも)　thigh or leg (of some edible animal)

monja-yaki (もんじゃ焼)　a slightly thinner, more watery *okonomiyaki* pancake [102]

moriawase (盛り合わせ)　assortment, mixed platter

mori-soba (盛り蕎麦)　*soba* noodles served cold on a bamboo screen [71]

motsu(yaki) (もつ[焼])　(grilled) giblets

moyashi (もやし)　bean sprouts

mugi (麦)　wheat; sometimes barley

mugicha (麦茶)　roasted barley tea

murasaki (むらさき)　soy sauce (sushi-shop term)

-mushi (-蒸し)　steamed

mutsu (むつ)　bluefish

myōga (茗荷)　a variety of ginger

N

nabe(mono) (鍋[物])　a quick-cooked stew [92]

naganegi (長葱)　leek

naifu (ナイフ)　knife

nama (生)　raw

nama-bīru (生ビール)　draft beer

namako (なまこ)　sea cucumber; bêche-de-mer

nama kurīmu (生クリーム)　fresh cream or whipped cream

namazu (鯰)　catfish

nameko (なめこ)　tiny smooth mushrooms used in soups

nanban (南蛮)　cooked with leeks (usually said of noodle dishes)

nashi (梨)　Japanese pear

nasu (茄子)　eggplant (aubergine)

nattō (納豆)　sticky, fermented soybeans

negi (葱)　leek (Welsh onion)

nerimono (練物)　fish-paste products

nigai (苦い)　bitter-tasting

nigiri-zushi (にぎり寿司)　raw fish pieces over rice fingers [54]

nihon-shu (日本酒)　Japanese rice wine (saké) [156]

nikomi (煮込み)　slowly stewed foods

niku (肉)　generic term for any type of meat

nikuman (肉饅)　Chinese-style meat-filled steamed bun

nimono (煮物)　stewed foods; vegetables simmered in a soy-and-saké-based sauce

ninjin (人参)　carrot; also used to mean ginseng (which in Japanese is called *Chōsen ninjin*, ''Korean carrot'')

ninniku (にんにく)　garlic

ninniku no kuki (にんにくの茎)　garlic stems

nira (韮)　leek (scallion)

nishin (鰊)　herring

nitsuke (煮つけ)　vegetables or fish boiled or stewed in soy sauce

nomimono (飲み物)　beverage

nomiya (飲み屋)　drinking place; pub-style restaurant [154]

noren (のれん)　entrance curtain [29]

nori (海苔)　dried laver (seaweed); usually used in sheet form [27]

nuka (糠)　rice bran (used to pickle vegetables)

-nuta (-ぬた)　vinegared fish served with *miso* and chopped green onions (scallions)

O

Note: The initial letter ''o'' is often an honorific prefix in Japanese (as in *ocha*). If you don't find a word in the ''o'' section below, check under the second letter of the word.

oden (おでん)　fish cakes and vegetables simmered in broth [99]

ōdoburu (オードブル)　hors d'oeuvres

odori (おどり)　shrimp served live, usually in a sushi shop; a variation known as ''drunken shrimp'' is also served in some Chinese restaurants

ogura (小倉)　whole pieces of adzuki bean

oishii (おいしい)　delicious

okara (おから)　a thick, fluffy tofu by-product

okayu (おかゆ)　rice gruel

okazu (おかず)　side dish

okonomiyaki (お好み焼)   egg-based Japanese-style savory pancakes [102]

omakase (おまかせ)   chef's choice

omuretsu (オムレツ)   omelette

onigiri (おにぎり)   rice balls wrapped in *nori*

onion (オニオン)   common brown onion; also called *tamanegi*

orenji (オレンジ)   orange

oroshi (おろし)   grated *daikon* to be used as a garnish

osechi ryōri (おせち料理)   traditional New Year's cuisine

oshibori (おしぼり)   small hot (or cold) towel [29]

oshi-zushi (押し寿司)   Osaka-style molded sushi [54]

otsumami (おつまみ)   snacks eaten while drinking [107]

oyako-don (親子丼)   chicken-and-egg mixture served over rice

P

pabu (パブ)   a small bar [155]

pai (パイ)   pie

pain(appuru) (パイン[ナップル])   pineapple

pan (パン)   bread

pankēki (パンケーキ)   pancake

papaiya (パパイヤ)   papaya

paseri (パセリ)   parsley

pīman (ピーマン)   green pepper

pōku (ポーク)   *butaniku*; pork

ponzu (ぽん酢)   citron vinegar, used as a dip [93]

potāju (ポタージュ)   a thick soup, or potage, usually made with corn

poteto (ポテト)   *jagaimo*; potato

puramu (プラム)   Western-style plum

purin (プリン)   a type of egg custard; the word seems to derive from "pudding"

purūn (プルーン)   prune

R

raichi (ライチ)   lychee (litchi)

raimu (ライム)   lime

rakkyō (らっきょう)   shallot (green onion); the term is also often used as a short form of *rakkyō-zuke*

rakkyō-zuke (らっきょう漬)   pickled shallots

rāmen (ラーメン)   yellow Chinese egg noodles [132]

ramu (ラム)   lamb

ramu(shu) (ラム[酒])   rum

ranchi (ランチ)   lunch

rebā (レバー)   liver

reishi (レイシ) lychee (litchi)

remon (レモン) lemon

renge (れんげ) a Chinese soup spoon

renkon (蓮根) lotus root

resutoran (レストラン) restaurant

retasu (レタス) lettuce

ringo (りんご) apple

robatayaki (炉端焼) a restaurant specializing in charcoal-grilled fish and other foods [114]

rōsu (ロース) ordinary-grade cut of pork or beef (*tonkatsu*, sukiyaki) [79]; marinated beef slices for Korean barbecue (*yakiniku*) [128]

ruibe (るいべ) a Hokkaido style of serving certain foods, especially salmon and whale, raw and partially frozen

ryōri (料理) cuisine, cooking; dish

ryōtei (料亭) a restaurant serving a variety of traditional Japanese dishes [120]

S

saba (鯖) mackerel

sakana (魚) the generic word for fish

sake (鮭) salmon

(o)saké ([お]酒) Japanese rice wine; any alcoholic beverage [156]

sakura-nabe (桜鍋) a stew made with horsemeat [93]

sakuranbo (さくらんぼ) cherry

sakurayu (桜湯) tea made with cherry blossoms

sandē (サンデー) ice-cream sundae

sando, sandoitchi (サンド, サンドイッチ) sandwich

sanma (秋刀魚) saury (fish)

sansai (山菜) "mountain vegetables"; these are usually edible wild greens, including a type of fern

sanshō (さんしょう) tangy Japanese pepper [62]

sanshoku (三色) "three colors": any dish with three different-colored ingredients or varieties [28]

sarada (サラダ) salad

sara-udon (皿うどん) Nagasaki-style hard fried Chinese noodles with various ingredients

sasage (ささげ) black-eyed peas

sasami (ささみ) chicken breast meat [84]

-sashi (−刺) raw (fish or meat)

sashimi (刺身) thinly sliced raw fish [54]

satō (砂糖) sugar

sato-imo (里芋) a type of taro

Satsuma-age (薩摩揚げ) fried fish cakes made from flour and ground fish

Satsuma-imo (薩摩芋)   Japanese sweet potato

sawara (鰆)   Spanish mackerel

saya-endō (さやえんどう)   snow peas

sazae (さざえ)   turbo shell

seiro (せいろ)   a bamboo basket used for steaming food; the word is also used to mean *soba* or *udon* served on such a basket

seiyō nashi (西洋梨)   Western-style pear

seiyō ryōri (西洋料理)   Western-style cuisine

sekihan (赤飯)   steamed glutinous rice and adzuki beans

senbei (煎餅)   Japanese "crackers," made of rice flour

sencha (煎茶)   medium-grade green tea

serori (セロリ)   celery

shābetto (シャーベット)   sherbet

shabu-shabu (しゃぶしゃぶ)   thin slices of beef quick-cooked in boiling broth [96]

shake (しゃけ)   another pronunciation of *sake*; salmon (usually salted)

shako (しゃこ)   mantis shrimp

shiba-ebi (芝海老)   a type of prawn

shichimenchō (七面鳥)   turkey

shichimi (七味)   "seven flavors": seven mixed spices, including black sesame seeds and red pepper [72, 85]

shichū (シチュー)   stew

shiitake (椎茸)   a large, flat Japanese mushroom

shika (niku) (鹿[肉])   deer (venison)

shimeji (しめじ)   a small Japanese mushroom

shime-saba (しめ鯖)   mackerel marinated in vinegar

shimofuri (霜降)   "marbled": said of beef or other meat

(o)shinko ([御]新香)   Japanese-style pickles

shio (塩)   salt [85]

shiokara (塩辛)   squid intestines preserved in salt

shiokarai (塩辛い)   salty-tasting

shirasu (しらす)   young sardine

shirataki (白たき)   translucent white noodles made from *konnyaku*

shirauo (しらうお)   whitebait (fish)

(o)shiruko ([お]しるこ)   a warm dessert soup made with *mochi* and red-bean paste [141]

shishamo (ししゃも)   smelt (fish)

shishitō (garashi) (ししとう[がらし])   a small green pepper

shiso (しそ)   perilla leaf, served with sashimi

shita-birame (舌平目)   sole

shōchū (焼酎)   Japanese distilled grain liquor [156]

shōga (生姜)   ginger

shōjin ryōri (精進料理)   temple-style vegetarian cuisine [140]

shokudō (食堂)   cafeteria; dining room [121]

shokuji (食事)   meal

shōyu (しょう油)   soy sauce

shūmai (シュウマイ)   Chinese-style steamed pork dumplings [133]

shungiku (春菊)   edible chrysanthemum leaves used in sukiyaki

soba (蕎麦)   buckwheat noodles [71]

sōmen (そうめん)   very thin wheat noodles, usually served cold in summer

soramame (空豆)   broad bean; fava bean

sōsēji (ソーセージ)   sausage

sōsu (ソース)   sauce; Worcestershire sauce [79]

su (酢)   vinegar; vinegared dish

sudachi (すだち)   a small citrus fruit similar to a lemon

suika (西瓜)   watermelon

suimono (吸い物)   a generic term for soup

suji (すじ)   fish cake made from shark

sukiyaki (すき焼)   quick-cooked beef and vegetable stew [96]

(o)sumashi ([お]すまし)   clear soup (without miso paste)

sunagimo (砂肝)   gizzards

sunakku (スナック)   a small bar [155]

sunomono (酢の物)   vegetables or fish marinated in vinegar

supagetti (スパゲッティ)   spaghetti

suppai (酸っぱい)   sour

suppon (すっぽん)   soft-shelled turtle or terrapin, often used in soup

sūpu (スープ)   soup

supūn (スプーン)   spoon

surume (するめ)   dried cuttlefish

sushi (寿司)   fingers of vinegared rice topped with raw fish [52]

(o)susume ([お]すすめ)   special of the day

sutēki (ステーキ)   steak

suzuki (鱸)   sea bass

suzume (すずめ)   sparrow

T

tabemono (食べ物)   food

tai (鯛)   sea bream

taishō-ebi (大正海老)   a type of prawn

tai-yaki (鯛焼)   sweet fish-shaped biscuits stuffed with red-bean jam

takenoko (竹の子)   bamboo shoots

tako (蛸)   octopus

takuan (たくあん)   pickled Japanese radish

tamago (玉子/卵)　　egg

tamanegi (玉葱)　　common brown onion

tan (たん)　　tongue

tansan (炭酸)　　club soda

tara (鱈)　　cod

tarako (たらこ)　　cod roe

tare (たれ)　　sauce (e.g., for basting *yakitori*) [85]

taro-imo (タロ芋)　　a type of taro

-tataki (-叩き)　　a dish in which the main ingredient has been pounded and is then finely chopped and served almost raw, especially horse mackerel and beef (like steak tartare)

-tatsuta-age (-竜田揚げ)　　chicken or other food first marinated, then deep-fried without batter

tebasaki (手羽先)　　chicken wing

teishoku (定食)　　a set meal, or table d'hôte, usually served with rice, pickles, and soup [30]

tekka-maki (鉄火巻)　　rolled sushi made with tuna

tendon (天丼)　　tempura-fried shrimp over rice

tenpura (天婦羅)　　tempura: lightly batter-fried seafood and vegetables [66]

tenshin-don (天津丼)　　Tientsin-style crab and egg over rice

teppanyaki (鉄板焼)　　Japanese-style grilled steaks and other foods [105]

teriyaki (照り焼)　　a method of cooking that involves basting food to be grilled or fried with soy sauce and *mirin*

teuchi soba (手打ち蕎麦)　　handmade *soba* noodles [72]

tōfu (豆腐)　　tofu; bean curd [26, 140]

tōgarashi (とうがらし)　　red pepper

tomato (トマト)　　tomato

tōmorokoshi (とうもろこし)　　corn

tonkatsu (とんかつ)　　deep-fried pork cutlet [78]

tonkotsu (豚骨)　　Kyushu-style pork stew with bones

tōnyū (豆乳)　　soy milk

torigai (とり貝)　　cockle

tori (niku) (鳥[肉])　　chicken

toro (とろ)　　choice, marbled tuna belly

tororo (とろろ)　　grated yam

tōsuto (トースト)　　toast

tsuboyaki (つぼ焼)　　shellfish cooked in their shells

tsukemono (漬物)　　pickled vegetables

-tsuki (-付き)　　including

tsukidashi (つきだし)　　hors d'oeuvres; same as *otsumami*

tsukudani (佃煮)　　Tsukuda-style garnishes for rice made by boiling fish, seaweed, and/or other ingredients in a soy-based sauce *tsukune* (つくね)　chicken meatballs [85]

(o)tsukuri ([お]造り)　*sashimi*

tsumire (つみれ)　fish balls made from sardines or similar fish

tsuna (ツナ)　canned tuna

U

udo (うど)　(spikenard) a vegetable stalk used in vinegared dishes

udon (うどん)　thick, white wheat noodles [71]

uinnā (ウインナー)　wieners; Vienna sausages

uisukī (ウイスキー)　whiskey [156]

umai (うまい)　delicious (informal)

-umani (－旨煮)　diced ingredients simmered in a thick, clear Chinese-style sauce

ume (梅)　Japanese green plum

umeboshi (梅干)　pickled *ume* (unripe Japanese plums preserved in salt)

unagi (鰻)　eel [61]

uni (うに)　sea urchin (the word refers to the roe, which is the only part of the sea urchin to be eaten)

uokka (ウォッカ)　vodka

ūroncha (ウーロン茶)　oolong tea

usagi (兎)　rabbit

uzura (tamago) (鶉[玉子])　quail (egg)

W

wafū (和風)　Japanese-style [121]

wagashi (和菓子)　Japanese-style sweets [141]

wain (ワイン)　wine [156]

wakadori (若鳥)　young chicken

wakame (わかめ)　a green seaweed

wakasagi (わかさぎ)　freshwater smelt

wakegi (わけぎ)　a type of Welsh onion; scallion

wanko soba (わんこ蕎麦)　*soba* served Iwate-style; it is eaten in tiny bowls (which you fill up as often as you like) and garnished with a variety of toppings [115]

warabi (わらび)　mountain bracken

waribashi (割り箸)　disposable wooden chopsticks

wasabi (わさび)　green Japanese horseradish [55]

Y

-yaki (－焼)　roasted, grilled

yakiniku (焼肉)　Korean-style barbecued beef [128]

yakisoba (焼そば)　noodles fried Chinese-style [103]

yakitori (焼鳥)   charcoal-broiled chicken on skewers [84]

yakumi (薬味)   a dish of *soba* condiments, including ginger, chopped scallions, and *wasabi*

yamaimo (山芋)   Japanese yam

yamakake (山掛け)   grated yam over raw tuna

yamame (やまめ)   trout

yanagawa-nabe (柳川鍋)   a kind of casserole made with eel or loach, burdock root, and egg [62]

yasai (野菜)   the generic term for vegetable

yashinomi (椰子の実)   coconut

yatai (屋台)   outdoor food stall

yōguruto (ヨーグルト)   yogurt

yōkan (ようかん)   sweet red-bean jelly

yōnashi (洋梨)   Western-style pear

yose-nabe (寄せ鍋)   a hotchpotch-style stew

yōshoku (洋食)   Japanese-style Western dishes [121]

(o)yu ([お]湯)   hot water

yudōfu (湯豆腐)   tofu simmered in hot water

yurine (ゆり根)   lily bulb

yūshoku (夕食)   dinner

yuzu (柚子)   citron

Z

zakuro (ざくろ)   pomegranate

zaru-soba (ざる蕎麦)   cold *soba* topped with *nori* strips

zāsai (ザーサイ)   a Chinese pickle: turnip preserved in salt

(go)zen ([御]膳)   (lit. a small, single-person dining table); deluxe-style

-zen (一膳)   a full-course meal consisting of a number of different dishes

zenmai (ぜんまい)   flowering fern

zensai (前菜)   appetizer

zenzai (ぜんざい)   a warm dessert made with *mochi* and sweet red-bean paste [141]

zerī (ゼリー)   flavored gelatin

(o)zōni (雑煮)   a New Year's soup that contains *mochi*

zōsui (雑炊)   rice gruel that can be flavored with various ingredients

-zuke (一漬)   pickled

-zume (一詰め)   stuffed

にほんりょうり
日本料理ガイド
WHAT'S WHAT IN JAPANESE RESTAURANTS

1996 年 5 月 1 日　第 1 刷発行
2002 年 5 月10日　第 6 刷発行

著　者　ロブ・サタホワイト
発行者　野間佐和子
発行所　講談社インターナショナル株式会社
　　　　〒112-8652 東京都文京区音羽 1-17-14
　　　　電話　03-3944-6493（編集部）
　　　　　　　03-3944-6492（営業部・業務部）
　　　　ホームページ　http://www.kodansha-intl.co.jp

印刷所　株式会社 平河工業社
製本所　株式会社 堅省堂

落丁本・乱丁本は、小社業務部宛にお送りください。送料小社負担にてお取替えします。なお、この本についてのお問い合わせは、編集部宛にお願いいたします。本書の無断複写（コピー）、転載は著作権法の例外を除き、禁じられています。

定価はカバーに表示してあります。
Copyright © 1988 and 1996 by Kodansha International Ltd.

Printed in Japan
ISBN 4-7700-2086-4

A NEW FOOD SERIES

FROM

KODANSHA INTERNATIONAL

THE BOOK OF
S U S H I

Kinjiro Omae
and
Yuzuru Tachibana

Foreword by
Jean-Pierre Rampal

"This book is as carefully and intricately put together as fine sushi."

— *New York Times*

There's always more to learn about sushi. This volume, in a convenient mass-market size, is jammed with tips on how to make these succulent morsels yourself, or order them like a veteran at a sushi bar. Learn to tell at a glance if fish is really fresh. Learn just what the sushi master's training entails. Learn just how good for you this dish really is. There's just one drawback: the more you learn about sushi, the more you'll probably start liking it. You may find sushi getting to be a habit.

172 pages, approximately 160 illustrations
ISBN 4-7700-1954-8

THE BOOK OF
SOBA

James Udesky

Foreword by
William Shurtleff

"Mr. Udesky is universally acknowledged as a soba authority in Japan, a rare honor for a foreigner."

— *New York Times*

The Book of Soba, now in a convenient pocket-size format, is the complete guide to making and enjoying fresh soba noodles. James Udesky, the first Westerner to become a soba master, offers the fruit of more than a decade of practice and study. Packed with easy-to-make recipes, useful advice, and fascinating accounts of soba's history and nutritional value, this is a book to be treasured by the home cook or professional alike.

246 pages, approximately 150 illustrations

ISBN 4-7700-1956-4

THE BOOK OF
SAKÉ

Hiroshi Kondo

Foreword by
George Plimpton

"A comprehensive guide to the world of saké: its history, ritual, where to drink saké, and recipes for food to accompany the favored drink of Japan."
— *Bloomsbury Review*

This handy pocket-book will set you on the path to saké connoisseurship. Follow this guide for correct warming and tasting, make some accompanying dishes, then sit down to a great saké banquet. Discover drinking customs, the folk-lore surrounding Japan's most popular traditional beverage, how the centuries-old "drink of the Gods" can be handily transformed into a Saké Manhattan—and much more.

232 pages, approximately 190 illustrations
ISBN 4-7700-1955-6